A Journey through the
Aegean Islands

George Galt was raised and educated in Montreal and
has lived in France and Greece. A journalist and literary
critic, he is now based in Toronto. His travel book
Whistlestop: A Journey Across Canada was published in
1987.

Contents

Haunt a valley where words settle into stone and the touch is evergreen. Relish the fruit of the earth and the circle of your soul shall be opened.

Attributed to
Pythagoras of Samos
6th century B.C.

Introduction

Up this way, up that, I climbed the winding streets of Naxos town one May morning under a cool, clouded sky. Away from the old harbour and the new beach hotels were laneways where you could escape the tourist-trade hucksterism that now dominated this island settlement. I was reminded of my visits to Mykonos and Paros eight years before. The houses were built in the same tight cubist forms, shoulder to shoulder with no spaces between. Yet Naxos seemed dull by comparison – grey and flat, as if my memory had etched a flattering gloss on the reality. Then the cloud curtain lifted and the sun emerged. I saw what I remembered: the dazzling, wall-to-wall whiteness of a sun-drenched Cycladic street, eye-stinging Greek light sharpened by the shadows of risers on stairways and by the dark relief of inset windows and doors.

A sleek donkey ambled down the stone pavement. In twin baskets slung on his flanks he carried two mounds of lime. From the fork at one end of the street I watched his bow-legged master empty the baskets at a house under renovation. The bow-legged man led his beast back toward us and then down a flight of long steps into a *stegasta* tunnel and out of sight. *Stegastas* are rooms built over the street. They shut out the sunlight for two or three metres, a momentary canopy of shelter from the sun. I sat on one of the white-washed knee-walls that doubled as street furniture and property fence. Ten minutes later the donkey's clip-clop echoed up through the tunnel and he reappeared carrying fresh piles of white lime. This animal, small handcarts and motor scooters were the only vehicles that fit the street. The public passageways of old Naxos, like those I remembered on Mykonos and Paros, were measured by the most common carrier of ancient island life, the hamper-laden donkey. With two coarse baskets as freight, a well-fed donkey passed through these streets with only a few centimetres grace on either side.

So much is recognizable, yet in eight years Greece has changed. The church exerts less influence, family law has been liberalized, and the economy has been mixed into the European Common Market. These changes amount to the piecemeal Westernization of Greece, a radical departure for a country that has been more closely affiliated with Asia Minor than with northern Europe over the past sixteen centuries. The new Greek family law, enacted by the socialist government that came to power in 1981, resembles the statutes of Sweden more than the old traditions of the Levant with which Greece was for centuries in tune. Membership of the European Economic Community, developed in stages since 1976, has been felt at all levels of the Greek economy. Government departments, for example, are under pressure to modernize their economic planning and revenue collection, and even in remote villages the owner of the smallest shop must now administer the country's value-added tax. Greece remains distinct from its northern partners, yet is now more open to their values and more disposed to modify its own traditions.

In the Aegean islands, where I lived and began writing this book in 1979, the most penetrating Western instrument has been tourism. Northern travellers have brought prosperity to many island settlements where the people subsisted for centuries on fishing, primitive farming and small-scale commerce. Those who saw the islands before the onslaught of tourism – even in 1979 many undiscovered spaces remained between the mobs of fair-skinned tour groups and back-packers – may regret the disappearance of the pure post-Ottoman culture of the Aegean. Yet subsistence in these rocky islands was too hard and the people too poor to allow valid grief at the passing of that way of life. In any case, the more remote villages still yield glimpses of the old traditions, moments when you tumble into a two- or five-hundred-year tunnel of time, though every year more of these tunnels are sealed.

Some say people are returning to the islands in large numbers, disillusioned by the congestion, smog and underemployment of the cities where they herded twenty years ago in search of a better life. I have met younger people with access to the tourist economy who have remained in the islands or changed their minds and returned. Tourism gives them a cushion against the cash-starved existence of their parents and grand-parents, and there are other compensations, the same benefits those who travel here seek – Greek sea light; sustaining food and hardy local wines; a tradition of self-reliance heavily buttressed by the solidarity of island society; and the knowledge that although the Aegean archipelago must qualify as one of Europe's bloodiest battle zones, humankind has prevailed here for as long as Europe can remember.

I have travelled to seven islands this year; two in the Cyclades – Naxos and Folegandros – were new to me and do not appear in the body of this book. I have not tampered with my original narrative, because we see with different eyes at different times of our lives, and because time refracts and distorts what has gone before. So my notes on Naxos and Folegandros appear separately in this brief introduction, and the rest of the book remains as it was, a young writer's first impressions of living in a foreign land.

We dipped down into the tight, winding lanes of the old market in Naxos town. Outside the stores stalls were spilling over with melons, oranges, nuts, dried figs and the fat lemon-like fruit called citrons from which the Naxian liqueur – also called Citron – is distilled. Inside the stores merchants were using the same tarnished weights and scales their parents and perhaps their grandparents once used. It could have been a spring day twenty or thirty years ago. The market bore no mark of the hasty modernization in the harbour – less than a hundred metres away, if you knew your path through the maze. Nor was there any sign of modernization when we climbed back up to the ruined castro. Marco Sanudo, having declared himself, under the protection of the Venetian empire, first Duke of Naxos, built the citadel here in the thirteenth century. Chunks of it remain, but these broken walls speak less of the Venetian period than the signs that curl over the castro's more distinguished residential doorways. In the worked lintels and carved façades of *arkondika*, as the elegant houses in the castro are called, survive heraldic crests and mottoes of the Venetian nobility whose descendants still populate this summit. One elaborate escutcheon displays a sword and quill crossed above an open book; on the book is cut a crescent. Over all sits a crown – the Duchy of Naxos ruling over war and peace.

Chiselled over the doorway of another handsome *arkondiko* are the words *Sustine et Abstine*, the Latin script as jarring in this Greek venue as the Arabic script I have occasionally seen on Ottoman ruins in the Aegean. *Sustine*, sustain, uphold. *Abstine*, abstain, withhold. Could this be a Latin equivalent to 'Nothing in excess', the inscription outside the temple of the Delphic oracle? Perhaps it also reflects the alternating generosity and harshness of life in these islands, the historic gyrations between poverty and plenty.

On Naxos, poverty must have been more the product of rapacious overlords and pirates than of any shortcoming in the island's natural resources. The next morning we rose early, collected our rented jeep, and drove toward Mount Zas and the interior valleys. A thick bamboo curtain grew on either side of the narrow road out of town. When the curtain broke, vineyards and irrigated fields of potatoes came into view. Reputed to yield the best potatoes in Greece, Naxos ships its seed crop all over the country. This rich, bowling-green lushness has few equals in the Aegean. Unlike neighbouring islands, Naxos enjoys both good soil and a generous water supply. Carried in tanker vessels, Naxian water fills the reservoirs on Mykonos in summer.

We climbed up out of the plain and reached the first inland settlement. By jeep Chalki sits only twenty minutes from Naxos harbour, but it used to be safely removed from pirates and warships, and so once served as the island capital. Walking through the silent streets I encountered an old man in front of a shoe store. Across the little plateia in another small shop sat an ancient seamstress who had lost all her teeth. Against the silence I could hear the hum of her treadle sewing machine. Most of the shops in the plateia and up the laneway were locked.

'Is it a holiday?' I asked the old man in my rusty Greek.

He shook his head and explained in a low, scratchy voice. 'The new road. The sea.' He waved to where we'd come from. 'They've all gone down to Naxos town. We used to have forty-five stores in Chalki. Now we have ten. Today if you want to buy a shirt. . . .' He shrugged.

'You have to have a car.' He looked at me doubtfully, then added, '*Morta. Capische?*'

Wandering through the town we found a bus tour led by an English guide. She was showing her group the Gratsia Tower, a tumble-down fortification from the Venetian period. The Gratsias kept swarms of bees and wasps, the guide intoned, and loosed them outside the tower walls when an enemy attacked. (How did they train these tiny missiles to fly in the desired direction?) We followed her down a flood channel to the village's ever-lasting spring. There a village woman was drawing two pails of water. A pipe diverted part of the flow to the public washbasins under an umbrella of massive eucalyptus trees. Washing was still done in the worn stone tubs, but the café nearby, where men once sat swirling their worry beads and watching their women scrub, was abandoned.

Back on the trans-island road the jeep laboured up Mount Zas toward the village of Filoti. Along the way hung heavy clouds of jasmine, invisible and sweet. Perched on a barren peak outside Filoti sat the miniature chapel of St John the Baptist – a whitewashed cap on a stone skull. Beyond it I stopped the jeep and walked into the fields. Down the mountainside grew olive and fig trees. Under the trees waved carpets of red and yellow poppies.

I don't know why Naxos remained unpopular with tourists until relatively recently. Byron was enchanted with the place and contemplated settling there, but for years the post-war travel boom overlooked the island. Writing only a decade ago Lawrence Durrell remarked that the groves and valleys of Naxos were for the most part unexplored. This is no longer so, though outside of Naxos town a happy balance has been achieved between accommodating foreigners and maintaining the integrity of local culture. As the proprietor of the rented jeep said, 'We are ruining only the town.'

Off the main road I found the village of Danakos huddled at the bottom of a crease between two hills. Here, too, the streets were silent.

'Some are out in the fields,' answered the café owner when I asked why the village was empty. 'And some have gone away. We don't have enough people here. I have no customers.'

I said I came from Canada. 'Yes,' he replied. 'I have a cousin who went there. To a place called Hollywood. You know it? Much money.'

I backtracked and continued on to Apeiranthos. It was early afternoon. Leaving the jeep in a square at the edge of town we walked into the maze hoping for some lunch. For generations the men of this town had earned their living in the marble and emery mines nearby. You see this heritage as you enter the narrow streets. They are paved with slabs of marble, and marble has been cut for exterior steps leading up to some of the houses.

An elderly couple beckoned from within when I paused at a taverna. Food was piled on plates on one of the tables: olives, tomatoes, a spinach and rice casserole, bread and cheese.

'We'll have what's on the table,' I said.

The old woman nodded gravely and brought fresh plates of tomatoes, olives, bread and cheese. From what I took to be the display table she lifted the prepared spinach and rice dish, carried it over to us, and made a little bow with her head. Then she and her husband sat down and began eating the display, which was not that at all, but their lunch, from which we had just taken one of the two main dishes. The other was a small bowl of stewed meat. When the old man saw me looking at his table – I was thinking that Greek hospitality is excessively generous; there was no need for them to give us part of their lunch – he must have thought I was envying him his bowl of meat. He picked up the bowl, strode over and insisted on feeding my companion and me a mouthful of meat from his fork.

As I had approached this white hill town I had sighted a Venetian tower near the summit. On each corner it sprouted the ornamental Naxian turrets that looked like four-pronged molars. When I paid the bill for lunch I asked the old man how to find the tower.

'At the top,' he said. 'Mr Zevgolis owns it. He has made it his house.' Apeiranthos, like many of the old Cycladic villages, was built in a labyrinth of twists and turns to foil marauders. Saying a house was 'at the top' was less a direction than a riddle. I searched for an hour through this marble-floored, fairy-tale place, and climbed up many streets that deposited me back into intersections I'd already crossed. It began to feel like a child's game, and a verse formed in my mind:

> Through the town
> we go
> up and down and
> around and around
> looking for the house
> that couldn't be found

We did find it at last, though no Mr Zevgolis was on hand to complete the fantasy and invite us into his renovated tower for a cool drink.

Later, as I drove back from a swim at Apollon, the fishing village at the far end of the island, a stout peasant woman waved me down. I pulled her, with her two bags full of leafy greens, up into the jeep. Her thorny hand, tattooed with dirt, felt like the root of one of the vines she had been tending.

'Me, I'm seventy-three,' she said. 'I've been working my fields all day.' Around us were the lush terraces of the Naxian interior. In ancient times over 100,000 people inhabited the island, and every square metre of arable land was needed to feed the population, six times what it has dwindled to now. Vertical farms hacked out of the fertile mountainsides covered the interior. The sturdy terraces have lasted for hundreds of years and some, like the ones owned by this old woman, are still in use. Yet the income from such family farms has never been large. Abandoned piecemeal, many of these gigantic green staircases have gone back to grass and wildflowers – the poppies and daisies flourish on them. So does yellow broom. Once we passed a colour-washed saw-tooth hillside that could have been a flower-box garden built by the local mountain gods.

Naxos displays little of its inner greenness to the passing ship. As we left, steaming up the Naxian coast in the *Limnos*, there appeared to be more agriculture on board than on shore. In the hold stood five trucks loaded with vegetables. Two of them rolled off at Ios, a small island overtaken by tourism in the sixties. We paused at Sikinos where a few passengers clambered down into a local caique and crossed the shallow harbour to the town's landing stage. In the dusk the *Limnos* ploughed southwest to our next island. It emerged as a silhouette of humps and crags in which three beads of light were buried.

I had wanted to visit Folegandros since reading that the yachtsman-author Ernle Bradford, who wrote the *Companion Guide to the Greek Islands*, was twice turned away by wind from the island's harbours, and so could not give a first-hand account of the place. The northerly *meltemi* which chop up the seas around all the Cyclades are especially treacherous around Folegandros. Arriving in a high wind, the *Limnos* too had difficulty mooring a main pier. The tieline made good purchase on one bol but as the ship manoeuvred to land a second rope, the first one worked itself free. We made a second and then a third pass at the pier, our hull heaving as if the *Limnos* were about to retch with the same sudden eruption that had come from several of its passengers. Still lurching danger-ously, the vessel was secured with two lines on the third pass and we were instructed to jump in twos and threes from the boat's landing ramp as it rolled down close to the concrete pier. On the fourth roll the last pedestrian disembarked, leaping into a sea-sprayed darkness broken only by the few dim pools of light on shore and a beam from the mouth of the ship. The truck and the motor scooter ticketed to Folegandros were victims of the weather, forced to continue with the *Limnos* to the next island; if the wind blew all night they likely found themselves in Athens the next day.

Folegandros (the accent falls on the second syllable) is said to derive from the Phoenician word for dry and rocky place. After walking the length of the island the next day I decided that the Phoenicians knew a 'phelekgundam' when they saw one. Water is scarce here. In the villages cisterns store rain. The hotel in the upper town rationed our water strictly. They did this in a blunt way that seemed to me characteristically Greek. When the proprie-tor felt her guests were using too much of the precious supply, she simply turned off the master tap for the rest of the morning or afternoon.

Folegandros rises sharply out of the sea, a bony spine with little flesh. Chora, as the natives call the main village, sits high on the spine at the crest of an unscaleable cliff. Not long ago this remote settlement saw few pleasure travellers. Now there are rooms for a couple of hundred visitors on the island, and when all the tavernas are full of foreigners at night Chora assumes a distorted theme-park atmosphere, as if it had been built as a tourist attraction. The villagers cannot afford to eat at the prices most of the tavernas now charge, so they sit on chairs and knee-walls in the shadows of the squares where they can watch the tourists eat under strings of naked lightbulbs by the kitchens.

At daybreak the Folegandrians reclaim their village. Women are in the streets with buckets, walking to the public water taps. Men are leading donkeys into the fields. The few little shops and offices in Chora are filled with Greeks. The tourists, when they rise, leave for the day to swim and sunbathe.

The morning I walked to the beach at Agkali I noticed the bus down to the harbour was full. A boat would collect passengers that afternoon and many of the rented rooms in Chora emptied as people prepared to move on. A hot hike up and down hills, the walk to the beach buzzed with bees and horseflies. Despite the scarcity of water, farmers were growing healthy vegetable gardens, fields of barley and, on terraces, vines. At the island's narrow waist, across which blasted the warm midday wind, a path descended sharply to the sea.

The beach was almost empty, thanks to the afternoon ferry boat across the island. Six bathers dotted the arc of sand. One couple lay naked on towels, and two pretty Scandinavian girls wore only their bikini briefs. Eight years ago nudity on Greek beaches was tolerated in a few places, but forcefully prosecuted by some local authorities. Now one rarely sees a woman with covered breasts at the seaside.

Shortly after noon a man arrived on a donkey and opened one of the beach tavernas. His competitor came over the hill on foot with a bag of vegetables on his back. Most of the bathers joined this last one. His tables stood on a high terrace overlooking the sheltered bay.

'Have some of my wine,' he insisted in Greek. 'Folegan-drian wine. I make it myself. It has no chemicals. And lots of vitamins.' This leather-faced peasant, his back slightly tilted from stooped labour and his hands gnarled from groundwork, looked indestructible. If there was any defi-ciency it was not in vitamins but in cash, which had to be why he walked several kilometres from the village of Ano Maria carrying greens to his terrace. We were his cash crop, a small one today, but in the high season he would draw a good crowd. The potato omelette, the plate of his homemade cheese, the salad of fresh lettuce, dill and onions, and the sweet Folegandrian wine, all from his own farm, made as fine a meal as I've tasted in the Aegean.

The evening light in Chora delivered the lambent tones I had stored in memory from Greek twilights eight years before. The sun, having slapped the land hard all day, now gave it a long, loving lick. From the hotel roof in this soft light I counted eight Orthodox churches. Below me on a balcony across the lane sat two yellow-haired girls. They were framed by a faded blue doorway on which hung a desiccated goat's skull. Beyond the village I could see the complex twists and turns of stonewall property lines erected over centuries to mark each family's terrain. Like the larger history of Greece, this record of ownership presented no rectangular grid. Byzantine and irregular, it traced the irrational scribble of dowries and legacies and clan disputes, and left them carved in stone on a hillside.

Now I invite the reader to turn a page and look with me at the islands of eight years ago. Greece has evolved and so have I. What follows is not what I would write were I to visit these places a second time. First impressions of a foreign land possess an intensity, an element of surprise and a clarity that may never again be achieved.

For me, as I lived then, here is how it was.

Crete, 1987

1

Samos

The light, she had said, pointing away from the dark harbour, only five minutes to the light. It seemed to me that she was pointing to a street lamp over a café several hundred yards down the main road. Fay and I picked up our luggage and followed the woman's brisk lead in that direction. She had met us at the steamer, one of a clutch of local people with rooms for rent in their houses. We passed the lamp over the café, and then many other lights as we followed the twisting road which leads north out of Vathi. I grumbled at every ounce in our bags, not to mention the typewriter, as we trudged up a steep bank to what she swore would be our final destination. And so it was, her high-perched house, on this road the last light visible from the jetty below. The five-minute estimate had been for helicopters, but we forgave her this piece of slippery Greek salesmanship as we rose in the morning and stood on our little balcony.

Spread before us is the Gulf of Vathi, a long deep inlet slithered between opposite ranges of Samian hills. This inlet runs a good three miles out to sea, so that we have the sense of being comfortably hidden away from the world. Its long finger of water ends here at Vathi, the island's main port. From our lookout we can see the old town crowded amiably on to a summit, and below, around the harbour, the sprawl of more modern buildings which now serve as the commercial area.

On the strength of a stunning view we buy food and lounge close to home. At dusk our lassitude is rewarded.

We walk up a dirt path behind the house. It delivers us on to a knoll with a clear sight-line up this arm of the gulf. For five minutes in the afternoon the heavens thundered and rained. Now the sky is suffused with a fixing violet light, holding the ancient Samian world still and timeless, brushing a soft purple picture of mountain and sea, with two small figures just now added to this out-cropping knoll. I do feel as if I am in someone's picture, perhaps my own, imagined, wished-for, but still unreal. I have been underestimating reality again. The world is often less noble than we expect, but not tonight. Tonight the world is built of magic poles and rafters all dressed in purple gauze.

A goat complains regularly nearby, and a turkey honks when least expected, at its pleasure. The sea below lies still as a garden pool. Up here and along the coastal terrain the greens stress themselves after the shower, the silver olive greens, the yellow greens of the brush, and a heavy basso green in the slender cypress trees. Everywhere the aroma of pine hangs, and occasionally a thick whiff of jasmine. Samos is an island entirely unlike the others. What strikes the eye sailing up its coast are the mountains, the rugged declivities and the dense greens, yet there are also hidden fertile plains. It is one of the larger Aegean islands and holds water better than most. At its eastern tip, the coast of Turkey lies only a few miles away. Partly because of this geographical situation, Samos has a past all its own.

The island's name is thought to derive from the Phoenician word meaning high, but few certitudes can be drawn from the frail evidence of early settlement here. It is later, in the seventh century B.C., that Samian history begins to take shape. A form of democracy was established at a time when the local economy was reaching for a new prosperity. Colonies in Asia Minor were founded, and crafts and learning began to flourish. A new warship was developed, spacious and fast, called the Samaina. No one visiting the island today can entirely ignore this period. Two or three Samainas may be seen afloat every night in any good Vathi taverna. The warship decorates labels of a popular local wine.

Democracy on Samos, as would happen often elsewhere, was only an interlude between dictatorships. In the middle of the sixth century, one-man rule attained new heights of local grandeur and ruthlessness in the person of Polycrates. His tyranny prevailed over a golden age when Samian commerce and culture reached their zenith. It has been said that Crete, Samos and Athens, in that order, were the founding fathers of the West. Samos has been largely forgotten as a formative centre, but its native thinkers still influence us. The most famous of them was the philosopher-mathematician Pythagoras, a contemporary of Polycrates. Others, who lived later, include Aristarchus, the first to suggest that the earth revolved around the sun, and Epicurus, a thoughtful man who has been demoted over time to the unenviable role of taster.

Polycrates established himself on the southeast coast of the island where he could command the Straits of Samos, a narrow channel off Asia Minor through which much of the ancient Ionian coastal traffic was obliged to sail. From this vantage point he was able to seize and plunder any passing cargo that fired his greed. The historians Strabo and Herodotus both record Polycrates as a maritime potentate unequalled in his time. He was, put simply, a merciless pirate, though a pirate with a fleet of a hundred and fifty galleys and a sizeable green island as his base. All of this would have made him no more than another successful despot, except that under his rule a rich local culture flourished. More interesting than Polycrates is Pythagoras, whose intellectual accomplishments are the great legacy of that culture. His influence, though modest at first, eventually pervaded much of the ancient world, and in some ways haunts our own. Anyone who has studied geometry knows Pythagoras from the theorem that bears his name, and many who are not mathematically inclined may dislike him for the same reason, and dismiss him as just another bore with a scratch-pad, or the ancient equivalent, a bore with a pile of pebbles. Pythagoras was many things: difficult, elusive, secretive, irrational, but he was not a bore, and his reputation is probably ill-served by the theorem. It represents a minute part of his work, if indeed it belongs to his work, a fact which some scholars contest. Although laced with numbers, his legacy is not primarily mathematical at all. It amounts to a philosophical system, or perhaps more fairly, to a religion. Some of the central ideas of Pythagoreanism are still revered today. Five hundred years after the philosopher lived, his doctrine was partly absorbed into the new religion, Christianity.

Pythagoras intrigues me, though I am not religious in any conventional sense. He is generally given short shrift by philosophy students now, Plato and Aristotle being the favoured Greek thinkers of our age. I would like to find time and space for him here on Samos, to travel back two and a half thousand years and spend some days seeing through his eyes. The philosopher himself might have shown interest in such an idea. He believed in reincarnation.

For now, though, Pythagoras will have to wait. We are moving down into the city, not his element at all. Our hotel is near the water, a drab concrete box with equally unassuming front and back doors. Its only distinct asset is Kosta, the owner, a well travelled Greek who retired here from the Belgian Congo when the good life for white merchants there collapsed. Kosta serves ouzo to guests at the reception desk every evening and relates anecdotes

from a colourful past. With his Greek-flavoured stories of
the pre-revolutionary Congo, told in fluent French and
laced with world-weary humour, he reminds me of a
shrewd, shadowy gun-runner out of Joseph Conrad's
Africa.

The town of Vathi isn't very interesting, confides Kosta
the first time we are alone. I have the impression that he
does not offer this opinion to all his guests. But perhaps
he does tell everyone, all the time cultivating the sense of
a unique confidence. Perhaps no one stays long here
anyway, so he can't lose. There is something malicious
behind his jolly exterior. Partly because there are so few
jolly Greeks, I am inclined to think Kosta wears a mask.
In any case, his assessment of Vathi as an uninteresting
town is not quite right. In the morning Fay and I wander
off in separate directions, she in search of olives and I to
reconnoiter. There is an Eastern flavour to the narrow
market streets with their cramped shops and frayed buildings. Several doors display a brass Hand of Fatima left
over from the Ottoman days. In fact, the whole town
appears to be left over from better times. I come upon a
public garden and wander in. It captures the ambiance of
all of Vathi town, slightly overgrown, decayed, seedy, yet
casually self-assured, as if there were no need here to look
sharp and seize the day, no need to polish surfaces. Long
sunny hours in this garden must unfold quite well without
coaxing and without discipline. A stray lettuce plant gone
to seed stretches its long stalk by the palm tree. Quail-like
clusters of feathers flap lazily after one another in the bird
house at the end of the path. All the long-leafed plants
here seem to be yawning, as if from a surfeit of time.
Nothing is new under the sun, they seem to be whispering, but many things are strange.

The birds and I are the only fauna in sight until suddenly
a woman in blue breaks through the stillness at one of the

gates. She is carrying a transparent bag full of fat olives. I remember her, I think. It seems we separated long ago, sometime before I came here to sit with these exotic plants. She is an apparition from my previous life, the one I lived in cold, snowy Canada for thirty years. After only a month Greece is changing me. Samuel Coleridge once wrote that good poetry should render strange the familiar. I think he would have liked it here. We chew a handful of olives, breaking the spell. I know who this woman is after all. She is travelling with me, and with any luck she too is changing. For a moment we talk about books, as we often do. Our map says there is a public library in town, and we still have time to see it before noon.

Across the harbour, in a ramshackle municipal building, we find the room. I thought we had taken a wrong turn at first. The building is blank, dusty and sad, the ground floor cluttered with packing cases and straw, a warehouse of some kind, but upstairs we are shown a room filled with books from hip-level to high ceiling on all four walls. Lacquered tables line the floor. The custodian brings us the only two English volumes in the collection. One is a history of Samos, the other a compendium of Pythagorean maxims. I would like to flip through some of the thousands of Greek tomes on the wall, but my ability to read Greek is poor. The Pythagoras book is very odd, self-published by one Hobart Hudson in 1947, line after line of sayings attributed to the philosopher without commentary or interpretation. This is curious, because scholars agree that none of Pythagoras' own writing has survived. What we have of this thinking comes to us second-hand from disciples and critics. No doubt Hudson had a good time crafting these maxims, but whether he meant to amuse the reader or edify him is unclear. Certainly I am amused to read lines like 'Green foods strengthen the teeth, give glow to the cheek, and aid elimination,' and

'Intoxication is the preparation for insanity.' Somehow they sound more like a puritan message from the American Medical Association than an ancient Pythagorean text, although it is true that the Pythagoreans were opposed to a diet of meat.

The custodian is shifting nervously from foot to foot. We have reached noon, but he has taken us under his wing, and once a Greek offers hospitality it is painful for him to withdraw it. He wants us to leave so he can go for lunch, but is reluctant to say anything. Almost no one here works past midday. Later, at four or five, shops and offices reopen. We rise to go, and he smiles gratefully.

We are bouncing on the bus to Ormos Marathacampos, which sounds to us like one of the magic towns created by Gabriel Garcia Marquez in his Colombian stories. The roads outside Vathi are very poor, and the bus is very old. We rock and crunch our way across the island, and we smell our way too, because much of Samos is pineclad, and within these forests the resinous aroma of pine penetrates our bus. On the softer slopes and slivers of coastal plain grow the much praised Samian vines. It is early June and the grapes all over Greece are in their infancy, but on Samos they already hang swollen with juice. Everywhere we see green, so different from Paros and the other brown islands we passed as we sailed here. Sometimes the driver has a newspaper or a loaf of bread to deliver to a waiting villager. Once he takes on a basket of lettuce for himself. It's a friendly, casual journey, but hell on the hide. After an hour and a half, we clamber down sore.

Marathacampos. We have traversed the island and are now perched on the side of a mountain overlooking a large, tranquil bay, the Marathacampian Gulf. Our bus turns around here, but we have six or seven kilometers to go to Ormos Marathacampos, the seaside village below.

We descend the mountain in a cab which, having no competition from the bus, overcharges us by half. Loudly I protest, whereupon the cab driver slides out of the car and introduces me to his friend the local policeman who is holding up a nearby tree. The policeman is dressed in the manner of an impoverished New York hood, but who am I to argue here? Whether he is the local gangster or the local lawman, I am going to have to pay, and I do, suddenly aware that inflation could swell the bill in a flash.

The few tourist places by the sea are mostly empty, but prices are absurdly high, so we try a little hotel away from the water. It's a dive, bleak and grubby. We take a room, then escape back to the bay for a swim. Several villagers turn a stony countenance on us as we pass, and when I nod and murmur *kali spera*, the evening greeting, their clenched looks draw even tighter. I don't understand, it's as if we are taboo. Greeks are generally quite open to strangers. Perhaps Ormos Marathacampos is only a sonorous name. Certainly the lower village lacks visual appeal: a few streets of simple stone and mortar houses, mostly tumbledown, the texture interrupted here and there by post-war concrete slabs. The pretty whitewashed planes of the Cyclades are far away.

As the sun sets we float in the sea off the town. There is an unpleasant odour hereabouts of something I can't quite determine. What? A suspicion tickles the olfactory nerves. I hate to admit my own stupidity, but finally there is no doubt about it. We are swimming in shit. The town must drain its sewage here. We should have walked farther down the pebble beach. Half a dozen villagers watch us unperturbed. Evidently if we want to catch the plague, that's our business.

We are looking for a village to ease the hot summer months, somewhere we might rent a few rooms and settle for July and August, somewhere remote like this place, a small hamlet touching the sea. Too bad the signs here are all wrong. After another walk through the deaf and dumb streets, we sit in a taverna behind our hotel and consult our travel notes. The only bus back across the island leaves from upper Marathacampos just after sun-up. We are developing a keen urge to get out. The taverna, the only one with food in the village, is gradually filling. By nine o'clock half a dozen tables are taken, some of them seating five or six. A group of rowdy local men are all drunk on beer. The other tables are occupied by an unsettling collection of foreign faces, deadbeats and desperadoes, international burnt-out cases, and perhaps a few secret lovers, all escapees from the outside world, or so it seems. The pallid skin and black hole eyes of one party suggest the damage of chemical overdose. Suddenly I have the feeling that travellers either come here for a day or two, or they come here to die. The fish, when it appears, is good, but already we know we will be rising at dawn for the bus.

For different reasons we left the popular island of Paros a few days ago. After two weeks of looking in the villages, it became clear we would never find an affordable place to live. The German mark had squeezed us out. But we did run into some worthwhile people there: the restauranteur Grigori; the madwoman of Naoussa; and Mary, a repatriated Greek immigrant from New Jersey.

We had poked our heads into one of the darker, smokier tavernas in the harbour of Naoussa, a small seaside village where we were staying.

'Grigori's place,' announced one of the few customers, and signalled us to sit, adding that the bouillabaisse was very good. He and his woman were Swiss, but spoke good English. How long had they been waiting for food, I asked hungrily. We could hear sounds of cooking, or possibly something more dramatic, filtering out from the kitchen. 'Grigori says he isn't feeling too well tonight,' our Swiss companions confided obliquely. A few minutes later I looked up to see the owner hoist a huge stack of plates into the air and drop them with a flourish on the floor. Then he chased his only waiter out the front entrance on to the quay, shouting insults at him.

Grigori stepped back in and addressed an alcoholic speech to no one in particular about his lot in life. Why should he do this work year after year, he asked the ceiling, when there were so many better possibilities? Why should he work for us, people he had never seen before and would never see again? The waiter slid back to his place unnoticed. I guessed from his tranquil demeanour that the chase scene was enacted regularly. When another table filled near us, Grigori shoved his pliable employee aside, grabbed two handfuls of cutlery and heaved them ten feet through the air into the middle of the newly arrived party. In a flash, literally, the table was set for dinner. No one was injured.

The bouillabaisse arrived an hour later. It was good. Grigori steered his way over to me, grabbed my spoon, lunged into my soup, and held a slurp in his mouth for a long time before swallowing. 'Not bad,' he shrugged finally. Then he pinched my cheek and gave me an awkward hug which damn near broke my neck. On the one hand tempted to leave, I thought also that if a man can make it thousands of miles across an ocean and a sea to unfamiliar shores, a single rowdy restauranteur isn't going to turn him away from his food. Hell, no.

Several tables finished the fish soup at about the same time. Fearlessly, our waiter cleared away the bowls. I was munching on a crust when the first flying apple sailed by me. It had been an unconventional evening so I took no more than passing notice of the missile. My mistake. An

airborne orange caught me square between the eyes.
Everyone else received dessert in the same way, on the
wing, but no one else was the object of such accurate aim.
Thus was Grigori's resentment of tourists conveyed to me
in the form of flying fruit.

Naoussa's madwoman. I hardly noticed her at first. She
was always about the village, but somehow didn't rise out
of the confusing flux of Greekness for the first few days.
Then, as we sifted the flood of images, the flood of
language, she slid into focus, Naoussa's single public
dissenter. Most visitors coming to these islands from
Western Europe or North America are struck by the
brashness, the forthrightness of the Greeks. At first they
are easily misread. To an outsider, they sound as though
they are relentlessly bullying one another, loudly and
fiercely. So there was nothing unusual at first glance about
an old woman in the street shouting roughly to passers-
by. It was when we saw her addressing nobody and
everybody with exaggerated passion that we knew she
was somehow disconnected.

She wore patched clothes from the days when Naoussa
still regarded fishing as the main local industry. And she
seemed to speak to us from that time. She was old enough
to have witnessed the pre-war dictatorship, the Nazi
occupation, the civil war, the restoration of the monarchy
and its subsequent demise, the brutal regime of the
Colonels, and now the new republic and the onslaught of
tourism. Perhaps more distressing than any of these
upheavals, she had seen the fish disappear. We couldn't
know which, if any, of these disruptions had helped loosen
her grip on the world, but I had a hunch that part of her
was raging against the large foreign presence in her town.
In any case, there was a remarkable contrast drawn
whenever she raised her sunken head and let fly with
invective at a surprised northerner. She was the only

Naoussan we came across who didn't give a ball of donkey dung about the tourists and their money. Did she have a message? I could only imagine her, tough, ragged and irrational as the sea, cursing us for stealing the smell of fish, for not rising with the sun and challenging the water for meat as the men of her line had done since their boats had first touched the island hundreds of years ago. She seemed to carry all the complex sadness of a modern Greek village in her tortured heart.

And then there was Mary. The day before we left, Fay arranged to have a drink with her in the harbour. They had met in a bakery over loaves of whole-wheat bread. Finding the bread, like meeting Mary, was an accident. The loaves were available for half a day once every three or four weeks before being baked a second time to yield *paximathia*, the rockhard crusts which fill huge cowsize baskets in Greek bread shops. The whole-wheat crusts, a breakfast staple, are softened by a quick dip in coffee. (Most other bread in Greece is leached white fluff.) Mary developed her uncommon taste for fresh whole-wheat loaves in America, where she lived most of her life. Her parents emigrated there from the islands when she was a child. Like many Greek Americans, however, she will die in her first homeland. Mary's husband inherited land on Paros, and so they retired to Naoussa, to a second life in a place lightyears away from New Jersey.

She lamented the winter in the village, icy sea spilling over the quay and eliminating the tiny waterfront square from use. Her house, she said, was unbearably cold. Happy with our company, and with the opportunity to speak English again, she bubbled on about the land she and her husband worked, about the local festivals, about her son in Athens, but every few minutes she would lean into the centre of our table and whisper: 'I don't want my husband to see me sitting here. He'll be real angry with me.' This was our first experience of the enormous power Greek men wield over their women, and I was surprised at its strength, even after all those years in America.

Mary was a strange combination of village naïveté and American street savvy. We talked casually, as if we'd bumped carts accidentally in a supermarket and stopped for a moment to chat, but every so often she would remember we came from another world and would pause to check her bearings. 'We're all Orthodox here,' she explained, describing a religious festival. Then she gave us a dubious look and added, 'You know the story, don't you? The one about the cross?' When we confirmed that we knew the story of Christ, she continued. I was left with the impression that Mary's Greek ethnicity must always have been a muscular shield in America.

She wanted to give us something, an impulse typically Greek, and asked if we had had good retsina. Yes, we'd tasted retsina, we replied, and it was very good. But was it homemade? No? Then we must try some of her husband's barrel. This turned out to be a complicated manoeuvre. Mary scurried out of the harbour area, whispering again that she must not be seen. In a few minutes she returned, carrying a small paper bag. She reminded me of someone en route to the doctor with a urine sample. When I looked inside the bag and saw the rusted cap and smeared bottle with its dense yellow fluid, I didn't feel any better. She insisted we try some on the spot.

'I promise you,' she swore. 'You've never had anything like it. It's as good as Champagne.'

Surreptitiously I filled the tumbler, then stashed the bag. Mary's nervous glances over her shoulder were beginning to reach me. What sort of monster was this husband of hers? My wife and I took turns sipping the homemade. It was marvellous stuff, full and smooth, with a pleasantly tart aftertaste. Any commercial retsina we'd sampled was ragwater by comparison. Suddenly Mary nudged me, half desperate, half gleeful. 'My husband,' she gurgled. I felt doomed for a moment, caught red-handed, until I remembered he had no way of knowing that we were at work on his brew. Mary introduced us to a harmless looking little man who said hello distantly and then moved off, not at all interested in two young transients, just a couple of the many thousands who will pass through the island this summer.

'Did you like him?' Mary asked expectantly. A bewildering question. All the time, I realized, she had been secretly hoping for his appearance. Her pride in him surpassed her conditioned fear. She had wanted us to meet her man.

There were good moments in Naoussa. I'll always remember its fine profile, a jumble of sparkling white cubes like an evaporated sea pool of perfect salt crystals, and remember too soaking in the blazing liquid of its bay, caught up in the strange wet fire that crackles across Aegean inlets under a noonday sun. But we imagined villages less crowded, and less expensive, farther from the busy mainland. Samos, we heard, would be better. A boat made the connection directly several times a week.

From Marathacampos, all the way back along the north coast of Samos: splendid peekaboo prospects of pearl sand and unruffled sea, and then, a few kilometres short of Vathi, we stop at a small fishing village. And we linger there a week. Kokari is charming, also relatively cheap. We swim in the horseshoe cove nearby, pass the afternoons with a book. In the early morning we can see the men unloading their pre-dawn catch on to the quay below our little balcony. At night, from the same chairs, we watch a lifted moon hang over the water like some magic spider's egg, laid orange, incubating white, enormous and potent, fat with children of the dark. Maybe this is the place. Then again, maybe not. The only rooms by the month we can find are nasty little corners, and they are all overpriced. Besides, Kokari is filling with northern faces, mostly German to judge by what I hear in the cafés. In one week the number of foreigners here has swollen noticeably, and we are still a month away from high summer.

Vathi itself might not be a bad place to settle. I try this out on Kosta when we return there. He's doubtful, but promises to enquire. Later that day he tells me of two houses for rent, one at six hundred dollars a month, the other at eight hundred. He shakes his head, well aware that these prices are outrageous. Canada, the United States and Australia are the rainbow countries where generations of emigrating Greeks have sailed in search of gold. We are often expected to live up and pay up to that reputation of wealth, just as some tourists here expect all Greek men to be carefree, dancing Zorbas. The prejudices are reciprocal.

By way of consolation Kosta arranges for us to meet a Belgian couple who are seeing the island by car. We suggest a drive out to the monastery of Zoodohos Pigis. One morning the four of us motor up the tortuous road out behind the town and head for the east coast. An ancestor of mine, whose boat anchored here for a couple of days in the last century, wrote that in the forests around Vathi 'serpents of an incredible size are said to have been discovered.' We pass the carcass of one of these giant snakes, a lifeless zig-zag in the middle of the road, six feet long and four or five inches thick. The accidental reptile makes me nervous. I imagine for a moment that my ancestor's ghost has planted it there.

We wind up a little road to Zoodohos Pigis, Our Lady of the Spring. Perched on a Samian precipice opposite the ethereal Turkish mountains, a narrow turquoise channel in between, this remote shrine enjoys a situation strongly reminiscent of Symbolist engravings. The lissome snake-clad ladies of Gustav Klimt cannot be far away, asleep at the whispering spring perhaps, entwined in Samian vipers, or meditating in a fold of those misty Asian mountains. Turkey is so close that any minor Greek god could land a pebble on its forbidden purple slopes. We are at the farthest reaches of the Western world.

As one might expect, natural tranquility here has its predators. The monastery billets a handful of soldiers. Their small military base hides in the hills nearby, and Zoodohos Pigis serves as their lookout. Tension is always high between Greece and Turkey, but since the Turks invaded Cyprus in 1974, the Greek army and fleet have been especially wary, so wary that we are not permitted to browse on this strategic summit unwatched. A Greek soldier acts as our guide, and guard. He hangs back discreetly though, not pushing at all except when the Belgian tries to snap a photograph of the magnificent channel. *Ohi*, exclaims our surveillant sternly, and waves the camera down. No photographs. Then in a typically Greek concession, snatching a nervous look over his shoulder, he adds conspiratorially to me that if my friend wants a picture, he must take it quickly, perhaps from the hip. No one must see. Apparently it is less the invisible Turks who worry him than his own officer. I do not suggest he lacks fighting fervor, not at all. No Greek loves the Turks. But here and now, on this summit, the enemy is absent, there are no installations in view, no secrets to be stolen, and he sees no immediate purpose to the prohibition. Unless religious custom is at stake, the Greeks are rarely sticklers for rules. I like them for that.

We might as well talk out here at the end of the world, so I mention our national origin, a starter that usually elicits a list of relatives in any number of North American cities. The guard's eyes give off a spark.

'Makret Droodo!' he exclaims. I can hardly believe my bad luck. A hundred and fifty miles east of Athens we are, on a remote island hilltop, but even here the intemperate Canadian political wife Margaret Trudeau has beamed her tell-all smile. Our guard, who has read extracts from her spicy book in translation (they were serialized in the Greek press) says she has *mia kali kardia*, a good heart, and wants to know my opinion. My opinion is that Canadian chatelaines ought to stay clear of the Greek landscape. I'm mildly annoyed that the ubiquitous Margaret has followed us here, but I do not tell him that. I say simply that she talks too much, because that is all my Greek allows me. Strange to be reminded of this flamboyant media showgirl in a land of dark, demure women and traditional family ties.

We twist back down the incline and turn off the road on to a track which debouches at a deserted beach. The water is silky, salty, willowy and warm. We swim out past the weed beds into the smooth wet silence of the channel. Midday fire burns through the swathes of purple mist girdling Turkey's mountain peaks. Our soldier said that fishermen on either side occasionally resort to gunfire in contest of a longstanding dispute over fishing rights, but I still can't imagine peace reigning anywhere more absolutely than it does here today. I think for awhile about Pythagoras who is said to have favoured long quiet days in the hills, the Samian slopes above us, for investigation of the inner mysteries. There he developed his beliefs on the omnipresent soul, the metaphysical qualities of numbers, the properties of the musical scale, the rule of silence and the various taboos. I imagine him descending to this empty beach and silently drawing triangles in the sand. Out here in the channel the silence of Pythagoras still prevails. But we have company now. A paunchy middle-aged Greek and his portly wife regard us with great concern as we stride dripping on to the sand. I am not quite sure how to interpret their look, but my guess is that they think we've left our senses. Nutty foreigners, his face seems to be saying, and he lets forth a torrent of worried words, pointing out into the channel and then back to us. He is offering a warning of some kind, that much I understand. Is it possible the channel is mined? He says we are swimming too far out, and repeats the word *karkaria* over and over. I thank him and return to our pile of things where we have a dictionary. *Karkaria*, it turns out, are sharks. The Belgians express doubt, but I notice that none of us venture past the weeds when we take a last swim. My thoughts on Pythagoras are again postponed.

We will not, it seems, find a place on Samos for the summer, so we are making plans to move up to the next island north. Meanwhile, there is one more excursion to be made here, to the town where Pythagoras is said to have been born and where the tyrant Polycrates ruled, the ancient island capital, formerly Tigani, now renamed Pythagorion.

The town itself is a disappointment. It has been partly destroyed and partly rebuilt so many times that the streets lack any sort of cohesion. The tavernas along the fashionable harbour crescent are pleasant enough, and so is the neighbouring beach on the Straits of Samos where Polycrates used to raid, but there is nothing more, nothing except the famous tunnel. Pythagorion stands on a small plain sheltered by a range of scrappy hills. This situation offered Polycrates a measure of security, but could also have been a trap. To safeguard his flow of water from the posterior hills, the pirate king commissioned what some have called the greatest engineering feat of ancient Greece, the Eupalinion Tunnel. Almost a mile long, with sufficient height and width for a man to walk through it, the passage was cut under a hill nine hundred feet high. Herodotus mentions the tunnel in his *Histories*, giving it literary immortality, but after the Roman period it fell into disuse and was forgotten, except as a figment of island lore, until 1860, when a farming monk rediscovered one of its openings.

An off-duty soldier loiters about the tunnel mouth as we approach. The sun on this mid-June day is excruciatingly hot, the sort of heat that makes the shoes feel as though they are weighted with cement. Going down into the cool earth seems a good idea. The soldier doesn't think so, however. He tells us not to bother. He has been down twice on military exercises and was not impressed. As we begin down the steps he adds a parting shot. Last year the army had to pull a fallen tourist out by a rope. Curiosity still prevails over fear as we descend the dewy stairway. I want to know why all the guide books give space to this deep dark chamber. We grope along the clammy walls to a light shaft and then beyond. Blackness veils us fore and aft. My mind slips into nightshift, offering rats, bats, reptiles and predatory spiders. And then I remember the last time I was in this part of the world. It was 1963, the summer of a powerful earthquake in the Yugoslavian city of Skopje. The hotel across from mine caved in completely, burying all its occupants. So did many other buildings. Sections of the Eupalinion Tunnel have collapsed too, probably as result of similar quakes. I think I would like to see the sun again.

Climbing out, the body feels like a babe emerging from the birth canal. We take some hope of discovery from absolute darkness, perhaps the more so from subterranean passages, because so often as children we have wanted to penetrate the mysteries of the earth by digging all the way to the antipode. It is a complementary wish to that of growing wings, this digging deep, each a kind of supernatural release. The child in me would like to walk the length of the tunnel and step out in Peking. Perhaps it was the child in Polycrates who had it built.

From where we stand now behind Pythagorion, another landmark mentioned by Herodotus is visible. The remains of the great Temple of Hera, a desolate single column and some scattered blocks, stand at the far edge of the plain. Leave the old stones in peace. It is hammering hot today. One ancient wonder is enough. Soon we will quit this town, and soon the island. The spirit of Polycrates has survived well here. A sense of plunder is uprooted everywhere on Samos. As for its native philosopher, I believe I caught a glimpse of him below the monastery of Zoodohos Pigis the other day, but there is no sign of him here at his birthplace. Perhaps, if we are lucky, Pythagoras will reappear on Chios, the next island north.

2

Antecedents

When the Sultan Mehmet II overran the Greek capital of Constantinople in 1453, he decisively smashed proud Byzantium, a civilization which had been founded eleven hundred years earlier by the Emperor Constantine. In the fourth century this ambitious ruler had fused archaic paganism with emergent Christianity, thus lifting Greece out of the ancient world and into her second potent incarnation as the Christian inheritor of Rome. When the Sultan sacked Constantinople, this second glory sank to ashes.

With the exception of a few privileged islands, the land was put to sleep for three hundred and fifty years. Languishing under Ottoman rule, Greece forgot herself, and was ignored by her cultural offspring in Europe. Only Russia in the 18th century under Catherine the Great adopted a sly interest in the region. The Tsarina's imperial ambitions were increased by her subjects' natural sympathies for their fellow Orthodox Christians. Despite much scheming, her efforts to annex the Levant came to nought. It was left to the Greeks to liberate themselves, which they did over a long decade of war, beginning in 1821.

Many forces joined to nourish the Greek renaissance in the early 19th century. Decadent Ottoman rule; the strong position of generations of Phanariote Greeks at the Sultan's court; the spread of Greek mercantile prosperity; a network of wealthy and well educated Greek expatriate communities across Europe; these were all contributing factors. More intriguing, in all senses, was the conspiratorial Philiki Etairia, a secret society with prominent members in and out of the country, and the organization which co-ordinated the first revolutionary outbreaks in 1821.

Three powers were ostensibly ranged on the side of the Greeks against the Turks in the Mediterranean: Britain, France and Russia. Now contending, now co-operating, the powers were injuriously slow in organizing military and diplomatic aid for the revolutionary front. When finally supplied, their help proved crucial to the ill-equipped insurgents. It might as easily have been inadequate. While the Russians were bound by religious affinity to guard the Greek cause, Britain and France showed little enthusiasm, and would have been much less forthcoming with assistance but for another pivotal force in the liberation struggle: the philhellenes.

Around the turn of the 18th century, European travellers visited the Levant in increasing numbers. For the British elite, Napoleon's continental blockade eliminated France from the traditional Grand Tour, diverting some travellers to Greece. Byron, with his literary companion Hobhouse, made the journey in 1809 and gave it the stamp of fashion. Later, partly as a result of the published accounts issuing from these early travellers, impassioned European and American philhellenes flocked to the side of Greece against her Ottoman oppressors. At stake, many perceived, was the freedom of ancient Hellas. They supplied large sums of money, lobbied at home for the Greek cause, and bore arms on Greek soil. Some, like Byron, forfeited their lives.

In 1810, eleven years before the outbreak of the revolution, a great-great-grandfather of mine travelled through the Levant, Italy and Asia Minor. John Galt was then an unknown scribbler, though he was later to establish himself as a successful biographer and novelist of Scottish manners. After the journey, which spanned two years, his interest in Greece faded. He stayed far from the battle-grounds of the liberation war. I guess from his books that he was not given to such sweeping passions as gripped the likes of Byron, nor to such recklessness. John Galt was a skeptic, and so a natural enemy of fashion. The vogue in the 1820's of volunteering to fight for Hellas would not have attracted him. In any case, he was by then otherwise involved in two consuming pursuits – literature and pioneer land development in Canada.

An obscure philhellene, and one who gave no direct assistance to the cause of independence, my forebear was nonetheless sufficiently interested in the country to publish a book about his travels there. In the context of nascent European devotion to Greece, *Letters from the Levant* (1813) may have served lightly to air the flame of philhellenism in Britain, and was probably read by a few who later fought in the revolution. Without knowing it, Galt left a small ripple in the current of history which was flowing toward the fight for an independent Greece.

Letters from the Levant enjoyed a modest commercial success and allowed John Galt to consider himself a professional writer. Copies now are scarce; the book has been out of print for generations. Like most old trav-elogues, it deserves obscurity, though I judge it not badly written and not without historical interest to contempor-ary travellers. Since my judgement may be clouded by the bloodline, I offer the opinion of Byron, who said about the book: 'No one has yet treated the subject in so pleasing a manner. It is a volume on the subject of Greece which has not yet been equalled, and will with difficulty be surpassed.'

Byron and Galt met by chance in 1809 when both were in Gibraltar, and thereafter were friends, though never close. Following the poet's death in 1824 at the siege of

Mesolonghi, several biographies appeared, including Galt's. Published in 1830, his *Life of Byron* sold 10,000 copies, a bestseller in its day. It seems from the distance a satisfactory way to pay respects to an old friend. The relationship had not always worked so favourably for the lesser writer. Before the appearance of *Letters from the Levant*, Byron's opinion of my ancestor's literary potential was not high. In 1811 he wrote Hobhouse that 'Galt is in Pera full of his Sour Wine Company speculation. I shall look at him in Mycone (Mykonos) in the "Prima Vera". He sent me a Candiot poem for you, but being the worst Romaic and the vilest nonsense ever seen, it was not worth the carriage.' Having read some of my ancestor's poems, I enthusiastically endorse Byron's appraisal, except to say that it was excessively generous. John Galt's poetry should never have left his writing desk.

The Sour Wine Company speculation of which Byron writes is almost certainly a reference to Galt's commercial dream of a clearing house for British goods somewhere in the Greek islands. His plan was to circumvent the Napoleonic blockade of Europe by means of a trade route through the Levant. He might have succeeded, except that an established house of British merchants opened a Levantine post just as his own negotiations for one were closing. My forebear harboured grand mercantile ambitions. He seems always to have regarded literature as an inferior pursuit, although by the end of his life he had produced a clutch of good novels without ever making any mercantile fortune. In fact, a few years before he died, one of his unforgiving creditors saw to it that he spent time in debtors' prison. In a way, it was a fitting end to a financial career that had been plagued by failure ever since his voyage to Greece.

The shadows of time envelop almost all our ancestors. They are seldom revealed. Seven of my eight great-great-grandfathers have been swallowed by history, as have all their wives, but John Galt's presence is tenacious and will probably outlive my own. His novels are still printed and read in Scotland, and he is remembered in Canadian history as the founder of the Canada Company, a land development enterprise which opened up much of south-western Ontario. If he made no personal fortune from his Canadian adventure, he at least saw one of his grand commercial schemes come to fruition. He was, I infer from his autobiography, a little disappointed with himself at the end, although he knew he had worked hard at a wide range of things, and for a Scottish Protestant hard work was almost sufficient in itself.

More than once I have half-consciously wished that John Galt had been less prolific. I can still see all his books on a high shelf in my father's library in Montreal. As I look up at them, aged twelve or thirteen, and run my eyes along their obscure and exotic titles, I feel entirely removed from his version of the past, as if I were leaning on a fence at the zoo watching strange reptiles. Yet I know I am connected to this past, that it is my past, and so I feel haunted by my inability to plumb it. There it is, but somehow unreachable. Woven into these misgivings is a sense of awe at the sheer volume of his accomplishment.

It is easier when our ancestors leave only faint outlines, though never as interesting. Galt's shelf full of novels, biographies and travel books discourages me from writing, but it also challenges me. History is a burden, yet offers the gift of possibility. Now, when his titles stare down at me, authoritative and dispassionate, I remember that he too was once a young bookless writer with nothing but time and paper in front of him, and all the libraries of history towering behind.

He was thirty, ill and without prospects, an ambitious lowland Scot who had gone to London to get ahead and then foundered and failed. An early business partnership went sour, so he enrolled in the study of law. He was not wealthy, but had enough money for a few years of advanced learning, money probably given by his father, a successful sea captain in Greenock. When illness forced him to give up legal studies, he was left uncertain and depressed. Perhaps my ancestor, with the intense rationalism demanded by business and the law, was betraying his talent for fantasy. Certainly he had not yet found the balance between action and imagination which characterized his later life.

Galt's journey through Greece was a personal turning point. From it he took his first book and a renewed sense of well-being. He went 'in quest of health,' he says, as so many of us come to these islands still, and he returned with the quest fulfilled. His illness would probably now be labelled psychological, though the wisdom of his day knew better than to slice apart the mind and body and diagnose one as separate from the other. 'My health,' he wrote later, 'for some time did not improve, and those indescribable sensations which are ever attendant on nervous diseases rendered me often very uncomfortable, in so much that all my projects were suspended . . .' He was paralyzed, at a psychic impasse, and went to the Mediterranean for a breakthrough.

What course, I wonder, would young John Galt take in my world? The conventional cure now for this kind of malaise would be psychotherapy. If he had sufficient funds for study or travel, he could also afford therapeutic treatment of some kind. In his day travel enjoyed literary respectability, just as psychoanalysis and confession hold literary approval in ours. He was following the prescribed treatment of his time: visit the sea, leave workaday worries aside, let nature run its course. For the patient, maritime relaxation; for the writer, travel. In this he was conventional, according to the standards he knew, yet I cannot see him following the accepted conventions of my world. I cannot see him in the therapist's chair or on the analyst's couch.

Psychiatry has amply documented the complex relationship between mind and body, and we have specialists in psychosomatic medicine capable of explaining in detail how an unsettled mind can inflict physical havoc on a healthy body, yet we persist almost always in slicing the mind and body apart and treating them separately. John Galt, although pragmatic and worldly, and an adherent of the scientific tradition, would not likely have breathed easily beside this slicing up of men into treatable sections of mind and body, at least not insofar as nervous maladies were concerned. The belief in relaxed travel as a cure reflects the conviction that nervous maladies, or psychological disorders as we say now, require treatment of the whole person. One way to treat the whole person, and perhaps the only all-embracing method (despite the extravagant claims of many psychotherapies), is to prescribe a new life: slower paced, less stressful and, for the sake of any clogged recesses in the dream tissue, newly imaged. This was how life abroad healed, and healed effectively. The principal drawback, as with so many pre-modern practices, was that travel was available only to those who were financially secure. Another weakness, and here the uses of psychotherapy must be acknowledged, was that the patient had to be possessed of the minimum psychic reserves required to map a course and withstand the rigours of environmental change. An agoraphobe, a victim of anorexia nervosa, a schizophrenic, these will suffer equally in Montreal, Athens or London – no use to tell them to take a trip.

I think John Galt would reject therapy for another reason. For him it would be too self-centred a pursuit. To sit for hours looking inward when you grew up knowing that half the globe lay largely unexplored, this would seem faint-hearted and singularly unenterprising. The world was there to be shaped and discovered, and if you felt anguished, disconsolate, down and out, there was always the possibility that you might be able to shape or discover things more to your liking. It is this attitude, more than anything, which divides me from my ancestor. In the hundred and seventy years since he lived and travelled, mankind has discovered and shaped the world to such a degree that its shape is now almost frozen. Indeed, many of us feel that the earth has been overhandled, that we ought to receive it more and mold it less. Our difficulty is that this would be essentially a passive approach. Only in magic-bound cultures have we worshipped the earth and out of fear refused to control it.

Still, though my ancestor and I differ in our attitudes toward shaping the world, I feel a strong affinity for him. Similarities exist between us. I arrive in Greece at the same age, take a year, as he did. Bookless, as he was, I have written for periodicals, as he had. And I too have been ill. I come, as he came, unsure of the future and questing after health. If I didn't hawk my library, it was only because I hadn't one worth selling. Certainly I am as ready as he apparently was to cut loose from past regrets.

There is the unappealing possibility in this felt correspondence that I am only a crank chasing after a ghost. I hope not. The ghost seems worth investigating in this case, not only because I share some of his blood, but because he provides a genuine and lively link with history. The early 19th century was a time of ferment in the Levant, and Galt's book brings it alive. For me, certainly, there is the added dimension of personal antecedents; besides, an impersonal travel book would be a bore. I will bring his consciousness along with me and see what it can do for mine.

To see all the places he saw, to retrace his steps exactly, is not my ambition. What I want from John Galt is not an itinerary, but a perspective, a layer of history that might otherwise remain concealed. Some eras – Byzantine Greece was one – are fatally obsessed with their past. Our own world, most of us agree, is blinkered to the racing future, and as I wander through Greece I would like to remove the blinkers and gain access to the lost store of time which feeds us. I would like to feel a puff of the enormous wind which pushes us from behind.

'Of all the miseries of travelling,' wrote John Galt, 'I do think that one of the greatest is to be obliged to visit those things which other travellers have happened to visit and describe.' It is true that our impressions are coloured by those who have gone before. We may be disappointed by exaggerated accounts of the exotic, or we may simply have lost the edge of surprise. I like the irony of Galt's opinion here, which seems at a glance to include my use of his book, although we are, in fact, visiting two different countries separated by many generations of change. In any case, no obligations where none intended. I'll go my own route in Greece. His path and mine will cross, I know, but I'll not force myself into his footsteps. We have, after all, to live in our time, whatever we may touch from another.

3

Meetings

They call this place Chios Town, but it feels less like a town than a city, perhaps because we are coming from Samos where the settlements are small. Chios Town sprawls around and back from a busy, charmless harbour. We have come here on the strength of a paradox. The island has a reputation for indifference and even meanness to tourists. A shipping agent in Athens, our hotel keeper in Vathi, a casual acquaintance on one of the boats, all told us to bypass this place. So we came, hoping to find a dearth of foreigners, and perhaps some empty rooms by the sea.

The Tourist Police, whose job it is in this country to help travellers find accommodations, have not done much for us here, though they can't be blamed. Outside of the few hotels, there is only a scattering of rooms. They have sent us to a pension on the outskirts of town, not bad, but not at all interesting. The search continues. No one is able to help, not the café waiters, not the hotel keepers, not the shop attendants, no one. They are all a little abrupt here, as if to defend the local reputation for misanthropy. Our sense of adventure is flagging. Perhaps we chose the wrong island after all.

On our third day Fay decides to look in an antique store on the waterfront. She believes that people who like old things have the right instincts. And finally here the island opens a crack for us. The antique store is operated by a poet. We get along very well, he and I, in halting Greek, often halted to a standstill, but no matter, we wave and point and grin, and he gives me several of his books when he learns that I too write poems. Dimitri he is called, a small nervous man somehow damaged, so tentative and tremulous, so unsure of hand and voice, that I wonder if he is one of the unfortunate free-thinkers who were arrested without just cause by the Colonels. Many were imprisoned. Some were tortured. It is not a subject much talked about now. There is still fear, and besides, the Greek mind is so heavy with difficult memories that such horrors are accepted by many as inevitable.

The poet says he has a female relative who may be able to offer us space. That much I understood. Then he says slowly, using small Greek words, like a foreigner in a Hemingway story, 'This woman is the mother of my wife. There is a room in her house. An empty room. Maybe it will please you. Maybe not. We must make a time. You will see it.' A time is made for the following morning.

At the arranged hour we knock on a weather-beaten door not far from the harbour. A weak, muffled voice calls us in. Someone draws the bolt. I push the creaking door and peer into a cavernous hallway, dim and dank. No one is there. Then from the distance high above comes a faint murmur, and we spy a miniature figure huddled up on a landing. Two little eyes stare down at us. A tiny, limp hand hangs wrapped in a cord which crosses the ceiling on a system of pulleys and drops down to the bolted front entrance. I close the door and the bolt springs shut. The hand drops the cord.

'Bonjour,' she whispers. Dimitri had mentioned that his mother-in-law would like to practise her French. She beckons. We climb the long staircase and she shows us into a turn-of-the-century salon, though just which century is turning here is hard to tell. This is not at all like the spare, simple rooms we have thus far encountered in

Greece. Apparently we have chanced on the chambers of the local bourgeoisie. There is a polite exchange of snippets: where we come from, how long we will stay, why we chose this island, what sort of work we do. Not an unusual opening. All Greeks meet new acquaintances with a barrage of personal queries. I turn the questions around for a moment and discover she is an Alexandrian Greek repatriated to her parents' native island, but she is not much interested in dwelling on the past and returns to an earlier theme, poetry and art. I had said that I was a writer. Now she adds that she writes too; and from an old oaken drawer pulls a piece of her work, a death notice for the late Bishop of Chios, printed by the local press. She hands it to me, a message from the dead in this tomb-like chamber clogged with antiques and darkness. I feign interest, but obituaries do not touch me the way they do some people. I feel defeated by proxy as I look at a long life summarized in four or five short paragraphs. While we pause for the dead Bishop, Madame shuffles off into a dimly lit ante-room, whispering through thin soprano lips something about artwork. She comes back with a handful of stones and scatters them on the table.

'*Les choses me parlent,*' she whispers. Things speak to her. The stones are brushed with black and brown paint, their curves and nubbles highlighted to create the garish countenances of miniature ghosts and goblins. She finds the stones by the sea, she says, and discovers little faces in them. They tell her stories.

We follow outside to a concrete stairway giving on to the roof, and climb up. Here she shows us her empty room, an afterthought appended to the top of the house where it catches the full fury of summer sun. It has a small overheated sleeping area with adjacent plumbing, installed so that everything will be flooded if the shower is used. There is no refrigerator, of course. We don't expect one.

She is running on now about how nice this will be for all of us. She has her driver's license, she says, and we will go for drives in the country together. We will go up in an aeroplane too. We will? I decide she must be getting tired and confused, but no, she explains to us that she also has her license to fly, and will take us up for aerial views of the island. At home we imagined Greek fishermen with painted caiques taking us out for runs in the sea. A septuagenarian dowager with uncertain reflexes offering to pilot us through the Chian skies never occurred to me. I am intrigued and ask her how much she wants for the room. A ridiculously high figure is mentioned. More in response to the whole morning than to her absurd price, I shake my head in disbelief. She comes down a third. Invariably shrewd are the Greeks, no matter how well-heeled. We tell her we'll have to think about it. Of course, she replies, reflect on it, and when you decide, go to Dimitri.

Down in the street my wife says the room will not do. The woman, a spiritualist manqué, would soon unnerve us, and we do not really want to spend the summer on a roof in the middle of town. I agree, but with reluctance. I want to know whether Madame wears a leather flight helmet. I want to know whether she really does fly.

We sit in a café and discuss the accommodation problem. In Chios Town the central plateia, or square, lies a couple of blocks behind the harbour. Tables cover the concrete terrace across the street from a row of pastry shops and cafés, their white-clad waiters darting back and forth through traffic with trays of coffee and beer. Ordinarily it is a pleasant spot under these shade trees, a little arid and architecturally flat, but pleasant enough. Today it's no good at all, a poisoned wasteland. We are sour with room-hunting fatigue and with the uncomfortable feeling that we may have just played our last card here. It's too

late in the season to try one of the more popular islands.
There are one or two seaside villages we might look at.
After that. . . .

Behind me a chair grates. 'Where are you kids from?'
asks the voice, and I turn to face a squat little woman,
heavily made-up, leaning forcefully into our future. 'I
couldn't help overhearing your English,' she says. The
accent is New York or New Jersey. Her name is Katy,
and she owns a house out on the fertile Kampos, the plain
where Chian agricultural wealth is based. She spends the
summers there. Katy married a Greek from Chios and has
inherited the house from him, along with a clutch of
relatives. She is half Greek herself and speaks the language
easily. But she seems pleased with an opportunity to use
English again.

'What d'ya want to spend the summer here for?' she
snorts, astonished. 'I'm telling you, this island is nothing.
It's too hot! The people are all lazy. It's boring! And
expensive! You won't believe how expensive. And for
what? You don't get for your money here. It's not like at
home.' Katy seems to feel worse about the island than we
do. And she's not even looking for rooms. This is a
refreshing new angle after the sickly sweet encomiums of
all the island travel books we have been reading.

Curious about the Kampos, its reputation for rich
farmland and expensive villas, I ask if she has many friends
there. Has she heard of the Argenti family, one of whom
wrote several books about the island?

'Argenti! Sure. I know about them. Their house is
about five minutes from my place. Big! You should see
how big. There's nothing else like it here. Of course, the
old man is dead. . . .' Her punchy, gravelly voice trails
off, as if in silent prayer for a moment, a characteristic
Greek pause for the departed. Then she fires forward
again. 'Tell you what. Why don't you kids come out to

my house for lunch one day? We can walk over and see
the Argenti place. And I'll show you my orange grove.'

Now it seems certain that Chios will receive us well.
Perhaps there is an empty white cottage under Katy's
oranges. Or perhaps she has an in-law with a rentable
house. For the next few days we pursue this and other
fantasies, meanwhile checking out two leads that develop
around town; neither is any good.

The bus to Katy's house travels through the centre of
the fertile plain. 'The scenery of the Kampos,' says an
erudite local guide book, 'is distinctive and bears little
resemblance to that of other Aegean islands. The aristo-
cratic families of Chios built houses here on their private
estates from as early as the fourteenth century.' We catch
glimpses of the remains of these houses, but the bus is
rolling along briskly and there are high walls around each
property. The guide book says most of the land is planted
with citrus groves, and the high walls are there to protect
the delicate trees from wind and dust. To me they express
only the aloofness characteristic of most of the Chiots we
have met. But the walls are probably not depriving us of
much. A massacre by the Turks in 1822 and a devastating
earthquake in 1881 left most of the villas in ruins.

We debark at Klouva Skoleia, an old schoolhouse, and
follow Katy's directions down a dusty laneway to her
front gate set in another high wall. 'Hi-ee,' she trills, and
for a moment I have the illusion of coming for cocktails
in Brooklyn. The heat and the cicadas bring me back. So
does an old custom still observed in Greece, the bouquet
of flowers. Katy seems pleased with our nosegay. She fits
it in a vase, then shows us her beautiful antique house
with its majestic high ceilings and stately cane-trimmed
furniture. Outside, a rush of bougainvillea purples up by
the front terrace. A bird-house flutters with pheasant and
quail, and goldfish slide through the pool where a water-

wheel once turned. The overgrown garden lies in shade under tall pines. I cast around a shameless eye for the guest suite.

'Come and see the orange grove,' invites Katy. 'I hafta take George his lunch. He's watering today. Do you believe how long it takes us to water the orange grove?'

I shake my head in disbelief.

'Fifteen hours!' she shouts. 'Non-stop.' She emerges from the kitchen with a plate of hot stew for the caretaker who is irrigating the trees, and we follow down through the garden and through a wall enclosing the grove.

'George!' bellows Katy, 'your lunch is ready.' A thick pungent scent of marmalade envelops us as we step into the trees. It rises from years of rotting orange meat in the ground and from a scattering of this season's tiny fruitlets recently torn off by the wind. Katy explains that these little green balls will be gathered by hand and sold to the marmalade factory. The caretaker is visible now in the distance, funnelling water into a system of troughs. She shouts that his lunch is hot, first in English, then in Greek. He shouts back in Greek that he doesn't want any. There is no time for food, he says. There is too much work. She tries again, with the same results. And I see she is terribly disappointed. A Greek woman's traditional calling is to feed her men and children. Katy's husband is gone, and her children are at home in America. There is only the caretaker left, and he has no time.

'What can I do?' she says sadly, carrying the plate back up to the house. Feed us, I suggest to myself, though I know we cannot replace the caretaker whom this woman regards as her maternal ward. Still, she does give us lunch, and watches anxiously as we eat it.

Katy's matter-of-factness about owning a house on a Greek island sets me thinking. Where I come from, this retreat would be everyone's dream of paradise. She seems to harbour no romantic feelings about it though, none at all. In the winter, she says, it rains without end. Every road becomes an impossible bog. The cold eats into your bones. And so on. But no matter what she says, the place still holds out exotic appeal for me. We must be very different. I ask her how her husband made a living in New York, as if this could explain her jaundiced feelings about the island. In a way it does.

'We ran a restaurant bar,' she answers. 'Where Lincoln Centre is now. That's why I'm so tough.' And she laughs a hard-boiled laugh, glazed, I realize, by years behind her polished counter in midtown Manhattan.

'My husband wanted to come to this house to die,' she continues. They lived here for several years during his final illness. She tells us about coming back to the island to dig up his buried bones after the flesh has decomposed, a standard ritual of the Orthodox Church. The bones are washed in wine, then stored inside a case within a tomb.

Out into the deathly heat we go after lunch, the Kampos silent as a giant mortuary. Everyone is asleep. The dirt paths and laneways are deserted. 'Bunch of lazy bastards,' exclaims Katy, waving an imperious little hand around at no one in particular. The Argenti compound is not far. I want to see it, partly because of its reputed charm, and partly because of the learned works on Chios I found at the British Council Library in Athens. P. P. Argenti was a Greek diplomat posted in London, and a scholar devoted to the history and folklore of his native island. He wrote his books in English. I am hoping that he might still be alive, but Katy says no.

'I think the rapist is in Athens,' she announces. We have reached the Argenti archway. Her reference is to the regular caretaker here whom she suspects of unsavoury sexual practices. I wish she would lower her voice in case he has not left yet. We don't want to be turned away.

I ring the wheeled hand bell by pulling its metal chain. A circle of clanging is thrown on to the deep silence of this hot afternoon. We watch the heavy metal doors for a sign. Nothing happens, but the doors bear watching all the same. Studded with diamond-shaped rivets, these huge, rounded portals are painted a ducal blue, the soft, resonant shade of polished aquamarine that well-fed, mild-mannered citizens might associate with authority in their dreams. Again I clang the bell, but no one stirs. We walk farther along the unusually constructed wall. Eight feet high it is, with chiselled stone spindles inserted at regular intervals in the mortar between oblong stone blocks. This, says our guidebook, is the ancient Chian pattern.

When we return, one blue door is open a crack. I ring again and a caretaker appears, still rubbing his eyes. Katy explains that we are visiting from abroad and would like to have a look at the estate. The man welcomes us in with a warm smile. 'Not the rapist,' murmurs Katy. Here too is a sizeable orange grove, but also a vast labyrinthine garden criss-crossed by a grid of overgrown pathways. We wander along them looking at the flowerbeds strewn with weeds, the family busts concealed in vine-tangled corners, and the abandoned outbuildings. Near the entrance stands a stone image of P. P. Argenti, the author. An inscription says he died in 1974. Perhaps the property died with him. There is an air of *l'époque perdue* about this place. It is a kind of secret garden, deserted yet inviolate, as if the last Argenti had left one day, locked the big blue doors behind him, and thrown the key down a well. At the far end of the estate we chance on a small house built in the old Chian style, pretty but faded, and obviously empty. It too gives off an air of eerie desolation. I wonder if there is a half-hidden alcove at the end of one of these pathways where the ghost of the old patriarch sits shawled in his Bath chair, exchanging confidences with a ghostly plumed parrot.

'Is that the main house?' we ask the caretaker on our way back. Yes, he says, but no one lives there now. The old man died several years ago. His son, Pandely, comes to the island quite often, but stays in a hotel in Chios Town. We leave him raking dead brush, a hopeless posture here, and walk out past the decorated water-wheel and through the big blue doors. I feel as though I have just stepped out of an elegant poem to genteel decay.

'That's some piece of property,' says Katy, impressed by its possibilities. 'But the house was no great shakes, was it?' The house was small, we concede.

'I'll tell you a story about old man Argenti,' she continues. 'They say he used to have fish served to him at the table, served the right way, you know, because he liked to eat in style. But can you imagine what he did with it?' She spits an imaginary mouthful into the dirt underfoot. 'He spat out the bones – by his chair! Imagine that! With all his money, and he could still spit his bones on the floor.'

We leave Katy at her gate with appreciation for an unusual afternoon. It seems there are no rentable cottages in the neighbourhood, or none that she knows of. There is the Argenti villa, too much to hope for, and there are many other seasonally unoccupied houses, but their well-heeled owners are not in the habit of taking tenants. She promises to let us know if she hears of anything. Her gate swings shut and we are on our own again.

Some days later, in bed with a fever, my body has given up on the room hunt. Hundreds of tiny itching spiders who inhabit the basement mattresses of this pension have been occupying me, in both senses. I have spent the day pinching them, one by one. Somewhere on the island there must be better lodging, but we can't find it. My wife continues the search. She went to the northern villages today. It is almost eight o'clock now, and I am beginning to worry. Minutes later, she bursts in, tired and cheerful. She has met Irini, a young woman with an empty apartment in Lagada, a village by the sea. We are going to settle there.

4

A Benefactor

The village grows more friendly. My wife is giving
English lessons to a rag-tag group of children from our
street, and word of her generosity has spread fast. Wherever we go now the village children hail her with a smile.
'Yassou Fay,' they call as we pass, and then murmur and
giggle among themselves, perhaps because there is no such
name in Greek, and the word it most closely resembles in
their language is *fai*, which is the word for food.

Irini, our landlady, calls at the open window at least
twice a day to invite Fay out for a walk or upstairs for
coffee. We live at ground level in three simply furnished
rooms: a bed, two tables, two chairs. Irini lives on the
second floor of the house with her two small boys.
Stephano, her husband, is chief steward on one of the
transatlantic cargo ships and will not be home for many
months. She is lonely and pleased to have a woman her
own age living in the apartment below.

One morning in July I am sitting on our sun-baked
front stoop lazily watching the olive green carpet which
covers the floor of Lagada's little valley, when Irini rushes
down her stairs. You have a telephone call, she exclaims
breathlessly. A telephone call in Lagada generates about
the same degree of awe and excitement as a winning
lottery ticket does in my country. This village is a
prosperous one, because many of its men work as well
paid seamen. There are more telephones than in most
island villages, but still they are rarely used. When calls
come in, they are usually from husbands in faraway ports,

and they usually elicit shouting and tears in the street as the immediate family gathers.

My own summons is not so dramatic. I am almost certain who is calling, though I have never heard his voice. Two weeks ago, after walking through the Argenti estate, I wrote a note to the surviving son and left it with our phone number in Chios town at the hotel mentioned by his caretaker. In my letter I asked for a brief meeting to discuss his father's books.

Mr Argenti speaks perfect English, though with a curious Eastern twang, as if his mother tongue were Cantonese. He says we have made a wise choice. Chios remains one of the unspoiled islands. He is here for only a few days, but will be happy to meet with us. We set a time for the next day.

Fay and I have taken to thumbing into Chios Town because the buses run at awkward times and are expensive. The villagers think it very strange that we choose to take our chances with random passing cars and trucks rather than buy a seat on the *leoforio* as they do, but if any are going our way, they invariably stop for us. This day a dump truck from the small northern port of Kardamyla pulls up and we climb aboard, she in the cab and I in the rusty wagon. We tear along the twisting coastal road and down every switchback incline as if the old machine had long since run out of brakes. Lagada is only ten miles from the main town, but this seaside road, cut into bedrock the whole way, is so contorted by all the bays and elbows that it requires well over half an hour to reach the central plateia. Our dump truck driver apparently does not have half an hour to spare. It's a heart-stopping ride he gives us, but for me in the open wagon a beautiful one, the clear distilled light of mid-morning flushing over the enormous sky and bottomless sea and ricocheting off the rockbound mountains, everywhere rocks and light, rocks and light, with a few improbable hairs of vegetation standing bone-dry and blinded in-between.

We are meeting Pandely Argenti in the library. He wants to show us through. The Argenti family, we discover, are generous patrons of the collection, having donated thousands of volumes and underwritten the construction of a second storey and a new wing. The family scion greets us formally in the reading room, with a bow and lips to my lady's hand. He is a small, slight man with what was known before the First World War as correct bearing. The same age as my wife and I, in his thirties, he is somehow not of our generation. The Cantonese accent is appropriate, though accidental, the by-product of an education split between England and Greece, perfect fluency in Italian, and years living in Lebanon. Mr Argenti is amiable but aloof, a combination which comes across as Sino-inscrutable.

He guides us through the building, pointing out the Argenti book collection on the ground floor, the fine array of his father's historic prints (maps drawn by early travellers and scenes painted by early water-colourists), the manuscript rooms in the basement, and then the folklore museum on the second floor, named in honour of his father, who established and endowed it. The structure has been renovated recently at the family's expense, and reopened only a year ago. He describes with distant amusement the gala opening ceremonies attended by such dignitaries as the Prince of Liechtenstein and Madame Tsatsos, the wife of the Greek President. A cavalcade of limousines was ferried over from the mainland and used to transport his titled guests through the tiny streets of Chios Town. The local people, he observes with a faint smile, were completely baffled by it all. Mr Argenti lives in Rome, and regards his island compatriots as wonderfully good-natured but woefully unsophisticated.

The Argenti Folklore Museum above the library displays a collection of antique implements, embroidery, costumes and paintings unparalleled anywhere in the Greek islands. P. P. Argenti went so far as to have commissioned several shelves full of miniature dolls, each one clothed in the traditional costume of a different Chian village. The image of these finely tailored, multi-coloured dolls gives some idea of the rich sartorial variety Chios must have offered the early travellers here. Gazing on Mr Argenti's brightly dressed figurines, I envy those early travellers their precedence in time.

One room in the museum is devoted to portraits, both life-size and miniature. P. P. Argenti is here, as are several of his forebears. The Rallis, gilt-edged European bankers, and the Mavrokordatos, related to a famous leader of the Greek revolution, are also represented. A glance at the family tree reveals that everyone in this large room is an Argenti either by birth or marriage. Banking and revolution do not usually relax in such close company; but then the Greek revolution was a patriot's war fought by all classes together against the Turks. Karl Marx was only a boy of three when it broke out. There is something else incongruous about this family gallery. I like the portrait of the savvy old aristocrat who was taken hostage by the Turks in 1822 and then hanged. But the lush satin folds in the background of several of these likenesses and the faintly foppish air brushing the surface of others strike me as awkwardly placed amid the pragmatism and frequent poverty of today's islanders. The genteel narcissism of all these Argentis in the Argenti museum is disturbing.

Pandely, as we are now to call him, invites us to lunch with the staff of the library. He likes to make a party, he says, whenever he comes to the island. So it is, at one o'clock, the library closed for the day, that ten of us are transported in taxis to a taverna by the sea, our long table covered not with the usual sheet of grubby *plastica*, but with clean linen cloths, glistening cutlery, and for ballast, five bottles of Samaina white.

There is more talk about the Argentis and their estate out on the Kampos. The traditional Chian villa, its garden and surrounding walls, all that antiquity we admired when we visited, none of it is very old, Pandely is telling me now. The Argentis fled the island in 1822 to escape the marauding Turks. Their property fell into disuse and eventually into ruin. What was not destroyed by time or the Turks was demolished by the great earthquake. Pandely's father Philip was the first descendant, as far as he knew, to return to Chios in over a century when he came back in the late twenties. The story goes that when he found what he thought was his ancient family seat, he stopped an old peasant, busy working the soil, and asked him who owned the land.

'These are the Argenti grounds,' the peasant reportedly said, 'but no one from that family has been here for as long as anyone can remember.' Philip Argenti claimed the core of the estate that was still legally his, and reconstituted the original gardens by purchasing pieces of land from his neighbours. In the following years he had his intricate Chian wall and traditional island villa restored from drawings and prints he had inherited and collected. These structures, whose age-old patina I silently praised when we walked the property several weeks ago, were completed only in 1939. Somehow the Argenti walls will remain genuinely ancient for me, just as I first saw them in that primal noonday heat.

Although most of the Chian nobles who escaped the 1822 massacre fled the island for good, they carried the old loyalties with them. 'We call ourselves the Forty Families,' Pandely tells us, 'and we've always intermarried, both before we left the island and after. My sisters are the first in our family to wed outside the old circle.'

He says this without a hint of self-consciousness, as if family associations lasting three or four hundred years are nothing extraordinary. Suddenly I feel light-hearted, giddy, wonderfully free. No man should have to bear such long unchosen friendships. I am exceedingly glad that I do not.

Lunch is a long lazy affair carried on a flood of wine and a light sea breeze. The cook comes out to join us after we've been served with large quantities of keftedes, tyropites, cheese, salad, fish, steak, melon and probably other plates which slipped by me unnoticed. Like many of the men on this island, the cook is a retired sailor. When he discovers that we're Canadian, he slaps me on the back and bellows, 'Shuchill, I know Shuchill,' and nods and winks knowingly. Then he helps himself to a tumbler full of wine, which he drains at one go. Shuchill, he says in Greek, is very beautiful, but very cold. Eventually it dawns on me that he is talking about Churchill, Manitoba, Canada's far northern grain port on Hudson Bay, a place I have never been near. He worked for several seasons on a supply ship serving remote northern settlements. The cook is delighted to have found some common ground with me, so I don't press my unfamiliarity with Canada's higher latitudes.

A couple of Greek youths pass carrying guitar cases. Pandely spots them and signals the cook to see if we might have some festive music. The boys play here at night, replies the cook, but they might be willing to make an arrangement. Our host, who strikes me as a peerless arrangement-maker, murmurs a few well-chosen words and the boys sit down with their instruments. For an hour they play and sing, or is it two hours? Tides of wine are lapping at our table-legs, all of us adrift on mellifluous Greek folk songs and incomparable Greek hospitality, and then the tide turns frothy, we are awash in a sea of champagne, wave after wave of it, Dimitri the tenor librarian is singing, we are all singing now, even the two foreigners are singing though they don't know the words, don't need to know, these being Greek love songs, melodious yet grave, and possessing a clarity of heart that renders words almost unnecessary. I do understand fragments of the lyrics, and am struck by one line which speaks of a courting love so strong it matches the singer's love for his mother and sister. This is a fine Greek sentiment, rich, fervid and pre-Freudian to a degree no longer possible in the whiz-bang love-a-minute world I used to inhabit. Yes, and which world was that? The champagne is giving me the illusion that nothing exists beyond a rectangular expanse of soiled white crockery and singing Greeks. Someone tosses a plate and then another, splintering them on the concrete underfoot. The cook disappears and returns with an armful of unglazed earthenware designed especially for smashing, and soon more plates are flying on the terrace all around us; an old Greek custom I take it, which fits perfectly the mood of everyone at the table, our drunken wish for a few minutes of postprandial debauchery while the singing floats away on the wind.

As lunch wanes Pandely Argenti lights a long cigar and withdraws into a cloud of melancholy, the sadness of a party ended, of love songs lost in the ether, and then recovers instantly with the ingenious idea that we be his guests again for dinner, Fay and I; a great pleasure it would be for him if we would come, and I accept with alacrity, offering not even a token protest, except to wonder aloud how we will make it home for a snooze, which by now we badly need. Don't worry about a thing, he assures me. It will all be taken care of, and so it is.

A taxi is hired to take us back to the village. Glancing at the metre as we arrive, I am glad it was not my idea.

The driver says he has been instructed to collect us at nine, and leaves us by the church, a few steps from home. After a long champagne slumber we are out in the street again, and there is the cab ready to spirit us away. The neighbours are astonished at our newfound mobility and so am I, so is my wife, but we have no time to explain. No one, absolutely no one from Lagada goes to Chios Town twice in one day. This may not be good for our local reputation. On the other hand, our friends here half-expect of foreigners, if I may say it, unorthodox things, so perhaps we will be pardoned.

I am trying to remember what we have done to deserve this evening ride along the spectacular Chian coast. Part of the reason must be the woman beside me who sat at Mr Argenti's elbow through lunch and soothed him with her quiet charm. That is true. The other part, and to me the astounding part, is that we are also here because I am a visiting writer. In my country an obscure foreign scribbler who turned up more or less unannounced would almost certainly be given no more than a polite hearing followed by a decorous brush-off. By contrast, here in Greece we are received as foreign potentates. Of course I prefer the Greek estimate of my station in life, though I know it reflects an elitist view of culture and learning, a view which, when I analyse it, I find distasteful. But I don't feel at all analytical tonight. I am enjoying this ride immensely, and am relishing the thought of another generous meal. The great moonball is glowing a candy ochre, slung low in the eastern sky, and the earth itself has taken on a ghostly moonlit pallor. Our positions have apparently been reversed. This grey pasture land around us, so densely laden with rock, has become an off-white moonscape and that glowing sphere across the water wears the mantle of planet earth.

The aristocrat has gathered a smaller group for dinner.

A few of the lunch guests have reappeared along with one new face – Elefteros, the airport meteorologist, who says life here was dull until he met Mr Argenti. The only problem with Mr Argenti's parties, he adds, is that the weather office opens at five a.m. and the parties often go until six. My guess is that tonight Elefteros will be home in good time. The droopy mien of everyone who was at lunch tells me that none of us will last till dawn. Everyone is subdued and a little sad after the musical afternoon.

Argenti and I discuss Greek entry into the European Common Market. He thinks the Greek government is overly optimistic about this new venture. The Greek mentality is a century behind European thinking, he believes, and the Greek mind has an Eastern flavour which mixes uncomfortably with northern European straight-from-the-shoulder efficiency.

'The Greeks,' I hear him saying, 'are closer to the devious business habits of the Middle East than to Europe. There is still that fatal mixture of clever stupidity here which places a layer of rotten oranges in the bottom of every box. You can't do that in the Common Market. And the Greeks aren't going to change overnight. It will be a difficult time here.'

Argenti, a cosmopolite who knows the Common Market countries well, may be a more reliable forecaster than the politicians I saw in Athens. Somehow, though, his gloom does not infect me. The Greeks are an adept and accommodating people, and whatever difficulties they experience in their contractual link with the north, those difficulties will eventually be overcome. In the meantime, they are already poor. They have nothing to lose in the bargain.

We are feasting again tonight in the same taverna by the sea. The musicians who serenaded us at lunch are playing their regular nightly gig here, amplified by faulty speakers. The sound is a mess of grinding static and lacerating squeals, the kind of electronic noise available on Saturday nights in lowlife North American taverns, except that here the melody is recognizably Greek and the squealing can be taken as part of an Eastern wail. Pandely wants us, he says, to see some Greek dancing. There are no comers, so he orders champagne again and spreads the bottles liberally around the establishment, hoping to loosen any latent soft shoes. The champagne, he confides, flew with him from Athens. Beer, retsina and ouzo, the common local potions, do not in his opinion induce quite the same degree of levity. This is a man who likes to lay on a good party. He is telling me so. There were many memorable festivities summer before last, and very successful they were, arranged when he toured the island with a composer friend gathering samples of Chian music. Unbelievable parties, he says, shaking his head, and I can only imagine something on the scale of today's musical feast, but more riotous and ribald.

From the far corner of the terrace now a couple snake their way on to the moonlit floor, the man with arms horizontal and fingers snapping slowly to the beat, his woman easing around him in seductive rhythms, her swinging hips intent on drawing every last ripple of sensuality from this midnight song. Tall and dark she is, with dark haughty eyes and a dark defiant swing to her limbs, dark fluid movement around her snapping man. He is lumbering, not at all light, but he seems to know that he is here only to witness her command of the floor, which he concedes easily. Soon all eyes are on her, and she is holding the music for us, grasping it gravely in her arms and legs. There is no dance in my culture which can match these slow suggestive rhythms. The dark woman is dancing a sexual dance, an aromatic loin dance, without urgency but flowing with desire, a dance binding the flesh to its own natural graces. These rhythms bear the poetry of a time when limbs were sacred and dances were their sacrament. She swirls from another time altogether, this dark woman does, a time long before the advent of electronic sound. Then a bulging moon shone as it shines tonight, but on an earthen floor, and a flute and a lyre led her flexing thighs.

Unknowingly, she has granted Argenti his wish for dancing, and granted many of our less conscious wishes too. Others follow, moving not as well but with as much grave pleasure. Kosta, our host's man-in-waiting, guides my wife through a couple of lilting tunes, and then Stavro, our waiter, takes Kosta from her and engages him in one of the most spectacular and difficult of Greek dances, the *tsamiko*. Both men wrap a hand in a white handkerchief, one standing firm and immobile as support, the other executing a series of acrobatic twists and backward arcs, slapping his free hand to alternate heels and to the floor on alternate sides. Stavro manages these athletic torsions remarkably well, despite an ungainly paunch.

Time to go. Pandely is inviting us back to his hotel. He wants to play us his symphony. By all means, I murmur to myself. Play us your symphony. Then we'll fly to Venus. Nothing is impossible today. We'll have breakfast on a star. Bach himself will serenade us. But no, I'm wrong, it seems the man does actually have a symphony of his own. It is the result of all those parties two summers ago when he toured the island villages collecting samples of local music. His composer friend, who recorded the village trios and quartets, was then commissioned to write a symphonic score based on the history of the island.

The Chian Rhapsody this piece is called. Pandely and his man have found the portable gramophone and have set it on a table in the harbourside lounge of the Hotel Chandris. Elefteros the meteorologist is asleep in an armchair dreaming of weather. The others have gone home. With yet another long cigar in hand, Pandely is explaining casually that he rented the London Philharmonic Orchestra for several days to record the music and then engaged a studio for the mixing. Only a thousand copies are being pressed. He takes us through the music now, a traditional pre-modern symphony, not at all disappointing to my innocent ear. Each movement represents a step forward in Chian history. Despite this highly literal treatment, the score seems to hold together remarkably well. But then it is four o'clock in the morning and the champagne is flowing freely through my blood again. Everything on earth seems to be working remarkably well as we sit here listening to the Chian Rhapsody and watching through enormous windows the ancient harbour of Chios Town with its single harbour light blinking pale stripes at us across the black water.

The music ends. There is a taxi waiting. Pandely bows and clicks his heels. Elefteros wakes with a start. We float out on the memory of wine and dancing, and on the rare echoes of Mr Argenti's secret island song. The land is all moonscape again, and we are all alone on it now as we drive back along the coastal road, our two white headbeams testing the solitude of rock at every turn.

5

The Lost Island

We have settled on an island anchored in ancient history. Folk tradition has it that Homer lived on Chios, and we meet villagers who swear the myth is fact. Scholars concede that if Homer was indeed one man (or woman), he did come from this general area, the coast of Asia Minor or the adjacent islands. Nothing more is known for certain. Still, it remains an appealing tradition. Most of us do think of Homer as one inspired man, and a man must come from somewhere.

The island is mentioned in some detail by Herodotus in *The Histories*, written in the 5th century B.C. After the classical period, Chios was swallowed by the silent back-water that most of Greece became. It reemerged in the Middle Ages on the rise to wealth and influence and eventually, by the 18th century, stood without equal as the centre of Greek culture and commerce in the Aegean. We see little evidence now of this past prosperity. It is as if another island had floated here two centuries ago, a lost island of mythical force. I would like to recover a piece of it.

The Argenti estate and a few other crumbling mansions in the Kampos hint at this bygone wealth and power. Up in the northern villages we find no such lapsed grandeur. Lagada, where we have settled, is only a century old. The men here work as seamen on the transoceanic cargo ships. They are tough, practical people, and they have been exposed to the modern world. History is respected in this village, and most of our neighbours know something of the glorious Chian past, but not much of it survives as part of their daily experience. Only one formidable historic link remains, the Orthodox Church, and its strength is not peculiar to Chios.

We have found one other small window on the past here, the public library in Chios town, and we visit it once or twice a week to read P. P. Argenti's history books. The library, when the island was at the apex of its prosperity in the late 18th century, was the most important in the Levant. Established in 1792 at the same time as the famous Chian School, it contributed to the town's reputation as a seat of learning unparalleled in Greece. The collection suffered badly during the great massacre and the 1881 earthquake, and has since been restored. Very strange it is to find this well appointed, well stocked library on a small and, by modern standards, insignificant island on the remote frontier of a poor country. The most recent census puts the population here at 52,500, though it may well be less now with continuing emigration to America, Australia and northern Europe. Of this relatively small number very few are bookish – a handful of religious scholars and the schoolteacher in every village. Occasionally one sees a man reading a newspaper in the local café. That is their only attachment to print. When we spend mornings in this building filled with 130,000 books, we are usually alone with the attendants.

P.P. Argenti, I discover, wrote some twenty thick volumes on the history of Chios, an enterprise which must give the island the most thoroughly documented past in the Levant, if not the entire Mediterranean. Here, in his books, lingers the lost Chios of Byzantium and of the Sultans. Sometime in the 10th or 11th century Chian civilization is thought to have begun its climb toward excellence. The Genoese and Venetian commercial empires vied for possession of the island, but in 1261 the Byzantine Emperor gave the Genoese an edge. He awarded them harbour facilities on Chios as a quid pro quo for their support of his own dispute with Venice. The Empire had recently been fragmented by the delinquent Fourth Crusade which bypassed the Holy Land and attacked and looted the Byzantine capital of Constantinople instead. The Greeks never forgave the Venetians, who inspired this barbarous act, nor forgave their patron the Pope. (To this day the Greek and Roman Churches have been unable to heal the enmity left by the Fourth Crusade and the earlier dogmatic schism.) Stripped of many possessions, and ill-equipped to defend what remained, the weakened Byzantine Emperor gradually ceded bits of his realm to more agile powers. In 1346 the Genoese extended the imperial gift of harbour rights by annexing all of Chios. Genoa held the island for two hundred and twenty years.

Under the Genoese, Chios was ruled by a commercial company, the Mahona. Sometimes oppressive, but always efficient, the Mahona provided the island with an effective system of defense and the framework for a prosperous economy. Chios served as a busy entrepot between Europe and the East. One of the principal cargoes of deposit was slaves. The island also exported its own products: Chian wine (famous in its day), oil, fruit, pottery, cloth and, by the mid-fifteenth century, high quality silk; but the product which earned more wealth for the Mahona than any other was mastic, a gum given by the lentisk or mastic bush. Mastic resin was as highly valued as the rare spices from farther east. It was used as a chewing gum and breath sweetener and was a base for medicines and paints. Because the little tree flourished nowhere else, the Mahona enjoyed a global monopoly on the mastic trade.

The new Genoese and older Greek nobilities intermarried and otherwise co-operated as a single ruling class, although the original Mahona company stood firm as a closed association. P. P. Argenti sketches the background of the native Greek aristocracy, from which he was descended: 'The Greek nobility of Chios had its roots in Byzantium, whose Emperors had from at least the 10th century sent members of the most illustrious families to establish themselves in the principal parts of the Empire, and especially the islands. . . . Moreover, in the 12th century, as the Moslem invasions encroached . . . the Byzantine nobles were forced to leave their domains in Asia Minor and settle in safer lands. In this way, some reached Chios.' The Greek nobles were guaranteed all their former privileges by the arriving Genoese in 1346.

Set apart from this upper class were the burghers, the Jewish merchants and the serfs. The Jews, as elsewhere in Europe, were obliged to live separately in their own quarter. The burghers, mostly Greek, were unprivileged but prosperous shopkeepers and tradesmen, and inhabited various parts of the town. Out in the villages lived the farming serfs. Tied to the land, neither privileged nor materially comfortable, they were liable both to military duty and personal service to the Mahona. Chios was a model of medieval efficiency, unless you were a serf.

A Genoese colony off Asia Minor was vulnerable. Genoa was a relatively small city-state whose possessions had to be defended against growing Turkish strength. Around 1410 the Mahona felt it prudent to begin paying a tribute of gold florins to the Sultan. This tribute, or *kharaj*, would today be called protection money and was multiplied sevenfold over the next fifty years. The Sultan continued to squeeze the Mahona hard, and eventually they fell into arrears. By the middle of the 16th century the situation had reached the limits of tolerance on both sides. Finally, in 1566, the last year in the reign of Suleiman the Magnificent, Admiral Piali Pasha captured the island, installed a Turkish garrison, and expelled the Genoese. Only a few Italians were permitted to purchase their freedom and remain on their estates. All of Greece, except for Cyprus and Crete, was now under Moslem rule.

The Sultan accorded exceptional privileges to Chios, encouraging it to continue as a commercial and cultural centre. The Chiots were made exempt from child tribute, a hated obligation by which the Turks formed their elite Janissary army, all originally confiscated Christian children. As well, freedom of worship was assured and economic concessons were granted. Relief from duties on bonded goods was probably the island's most important commercial privilege, allowing as it did continued expansion of the shipping industry.

In striking contrast to the rest of Greece, the island flourished under Ottoman rule. It is generally believed that the Turks were easier masters than the Genoese. An annual tribute was required by the Sultan, but the resident garrison was small, and the level of self-government high. An Austrian diplomat writing in 1575 had this opinion: 'The Venetians kept their subjects in Cyprus, like the Genoese theirs in Chios, worse than slaves.' The conquest by Piali Pasha in 1566 had, to a degree, liberated the island. For the Chiots, Turkish rule meant a policy of benign neglect.

By the end of the 18th century Chios enjoyed a widespread European reputation as the one sanctuary of Western culture and learning in an otherwise desolate Moslem world. The population was estimated variously between 100,00 and 150,000, considerably more than it is today. Travellers' accounts painted the picture of an affluent and scholarly paradise. The traveller Olivier, writing in 1794, observed that 'the Chiots are distinguished from other Greeks by a marked leaning towards commerce, a lively taste for the arts, a willingness to engage in ventures, and by a light-hearted spirit, playful and epigrammatic. No other town in the Levant embraces such a wealth of learning; no other contains so many men exempt from prejudices, full of good sense and reason.'

The island became an obligatory port of call for educated Europeans on a circuit of the Levant. My ancestor John Galt stopped briefly at Scio, as it was then called (and sometimes Sio), in the spring of 1810, only a decade before the devastating massacres. It was a place he would not quickly forget: 'The City of Scio, from the innumerable villas, gardens, and windmills with which it is surrounded, and the trees interspread among the houses of the town, has the appearance of a vast village. The vessels in the harbour, the insulated light-houses and fortresses, and the mountains behind, abrupt and lofty, render the view one of the most beautiful landscapes in the Mediterranean.

'The island formerly belonged to the Genoese, by whom the present fortresses were constructed and its beautiful silk manufactures established. The houses are built in the Italian style, with lofty pyramidal roofs. The Turks having intermarried with the natives, the society is said to be more free in this island than in any other part of the Ottoman Empire. Except in the particular of dress and the streets where the shops are situated, everything about Scio has the appearance of a town in Christendom.

'The shops are well filled, many of them with those gorgeous stuffs of woven gold and silver which are but rarely seen even in London. Silks which rival in beauty and elegance the richest of France and Italy are produced in the Sciot looms. In one ware-room I was shewn brocades as neatly executed as more costly articles of the same kind come from Lyons. These valuable manufactures are sent to Constantinople and Grand Cairo, into the interior of Asia, and through Africa as far as the Court of Morocco.'

There is a curious reference in Galt's Chian letter to the reputation of the local women. 'The good women of Scio,' he wrote, 'have long suffered under an unfounded calumny from those travellers who represent them as so outrageously libidinous, at the sight of strangers, as to offer themselves with no more decency than the girls of London.' I think this must be a response to *The Total Discourse of the Rare Adventures of William Lithgow*, published in the early 17th century. Lithgow, whose own reputation was marred when he was caught compromising a Scottish lady (and had both his ears sliced off by her angry brothers), travelled to Chios and recorded the following: 'The women of the City of Sio are the most beautiful Dames or rather Angelicall creatures of all Greeks upon the face of the earth, and greatly given to Venery. Their Husbands are their Pandors, and when they see any stranger arrive, they will presently demand of him; if he would have a Mistresse; and so they make Whoores of their own wives.' Continuing this theme, Galt remarked: 'Almost the whole of the lower class are silk-weavers and embroiderers; and that earnestness with which they invite and even pull strangers into their houses arises from their anxiety to obtain purchasers. I went into several of their houses, at first with no very respectful idea of their manners; but I was soon set right, and convinced that the smiling vivacity with which I had been invited was the pure offspring of mercantile assiduity. The handsomest women will, no doubt, probably attract the greatest number of dealers; the freedom of the women in general is unquestionably not owing to any peculiar degree of licentiousness.' Perhaps Lithgow's sexual imagination had been somehow exaggerated by the loss of both ears. Or, equally plausible, perhaps he appealed more to Chian lust than John Galt did. Certainly the earless Scot left a reputation as the more ardent womanizer. My ancestor, so far as I know, was never chased off by any woman's brothers.

John Galt was fortunate to see the island when he did in 1810. Conspiracies were afoot in the Levant which would soon raze to the ground this remarkable little civilization. The Greek independence movement had already been stirring for some years in the European centres of the Greek diaspora. Cities such as Venice, Trieste, Odessa, Paris and London harboured large numbers of expatriate Byzantine Greeks who had emigrated steadily since the fall of Constantinople in 1453. By the early 19th century a strong revival of nationalist sentiment had taken root in these communities and was being exported back to the homeland. In 1814 a clandestine nationalist society, the Philiki Etairia, was formed, and in 1821 the revolutionary war broke out.

For Chios the consequences were disastrous. In the spring of 1822 a force of invading Samiots landed near the main town intent on liberating the island. Chios, with its agricultural and marine wealth, was regarded as a valuable prize by the Greek revolutionary leaders. The Chiots themselves, on the other hand, were not anxious to join the struggle. When sounded out that winter, Chian leaders had pointed out that the Greek fleet lay a hundred and sixty miles away at Hydra, the revolutionary navy's principal harbour, whereas Chios lay a mere two miles off the Turkish coast. They judged that any rebellion on their part in the early stages of the war would be ill-fated. The Samiots landed anyway, without agreement from the natives. Immediately on news of their arrival eighty hostages were taken from among prominent island families and jailed by the Turkish garrison. The Samian force camped on the table mountain behind Chios Town, engaged in futile bombardment of the impervious citadel, and then overran the settlement, fighting ineffectively and plundering Greek and Turk alike without mercy. The Turkish fleet, not far off, was alerted and sailed on the island. As soon as the Ottoman ships were sighted, the Samiots fled, leaving their stunned compatriots to fend off the Sultan's wrath. What followed was a massacre of such horrendous proportions it stirred the conscience of Europe.

An American traveller, J. L. Stephens, who visited the island some years later and spoke with witnesses of the debacle, described it thus: 'Women were ripped open, children dashed against the walls, the heads of whole families stuck on pikes out of the windows of their houses, while their murderers gave themselves up to riot and plunder within. The hostages were hung in a row from the walls of the castle; an indiscriminate and universal burning and massacre took place; in a few days the ground was cumbered with the dead. Out of a population of 110,000, 60,000 are supposed to have been murdered; 20,000 to have escaped; and 30,000 to have been sold into slavery. Boys and girls were sold publicly in Smyrna and Constantinople at a dollar a head.' There is disagreement among scholars about the precise number of dead and fugitive Chiots left by these atrocities, but if the second bloodbath is included Stephens is not far off most estimates. Two months later, in retaliation for a brace of fireships introduced into the Sultan's fleet moored off the island, his troops burned twenty-one mastic villages, previously spared for their economic value, and slaughtered all their inhabitants.

When he travelled to the island seventeen years after the massacre, Stephens confronted a depressing scene. The mantle of charm worn by old Chios had been seized and destroyed. 'The town,' he wrote, 'was a complete mass of ruins; the walls of many fine buildings were still standing, crumbling to pieces, and still black with the fire of the incendiary Turks. The town that had grown up upon the ruins consisted of a row of miserable shanties, occupied as shops for the mere necessities of life, where the shopman slept on his window-shutter in front.'

For Chios 1822 marked the end of a lush flowering. For revolutionary Greece as a whole, however, the island massacre turned out to be less a black tragedy than an elegant plea for help. Enlightened Europeans were outraged by the wanton destruction of this little paradise which had been immortalized in so many French and English travel accounts. Eugene Delacroix's rendering of the slaughter was widely adopted as a talisman, a moving symbol of the horror felt by philhellenes everywhere. The end of Chios provoked first a mournful wail and then a battle cry. It was a turning point for anti-Ottoman sentiment abroad, and so was instrumental in the liberation of Greece.

Chios never regained its former splendour, partly because of irreparable physical havoc and partly because the War of Independence had altered the old social structure. Then came a final blow. What few economic gains had been made in the post-war period were again lost in the devastating earthquake of 1881. H. F. Tozer, a traveller who visited five years after the quake, observed that the country districts were a scene of universal ruin, and noted that, although the main town was partly rebuilt, damage to it had been severe. A contemporary newspaper report described the after-math: 'The town looks as if it had been subjected to a terrible bombardment; hundreds of houses have been transformed into a shapeless mass of ruins, under which lie buried an unknown number of victims.' Loss of life was heavy and, except for a few southern villages, whatever buildings had survived the Turks' vengeance unscathed were now badly mangled by nature.

Even today Chiots live in awe of the massacres and the earthquake. Children recount the stories as if they had happened yesterday. Although a hundred years have passed, and two world wars, it is to the events of the 19th century and earlier that these people look when they think of history. The Turkish era lasted longer on the island than it did for most of the rest of the country and perhaps kept alive memories of the slaughter. Not until the Balkan War in 1912 was Chios finally liberated and united with Greece. There are many contemporary islanders whose parents or grandparents lived under Turkish rule, and the very old remember learning essential Turkish phrases as well as their native Greek. The earthquake, not so distant in time, is well remembered, and often with a hint of wariness, perhaps because the people here believe the earth may shake again.

It is sad to contemplate this once-upon-a-time island trampled by man and nature. The 20th century has handed us atrocities of such immense proportions that mass killings now seem a commonplace of history, an inevitable human flaw. Of course that is false, a perilous view and a distortion. It leaves us without feeling for the tortured and the dead. Here on this island, a small world unto itself holding the rest of the world at bay, it is somehow easier to admit the reality of this or any massacre. The obstacles to perception are lifted a little here. As we walk from the library, a smell rises of curdled blood shed in the slanting streets. Heads stare from the pike fences above us, and bodies hang naked from trees. The Turks rear on stained horses, wrenching dumbstruck children from the catatonic arms of their mothers, and Ottoman swords slice through human members as easily as a blade severs silk. There are charred moaning bodies, slashed bodies, faces frozen in fright. They have cast a liquid red gloom over this island, most strongly felt, not when the sky is grey, but when the sun presses all its smothering weight in the first hour following noon. If you listen, you can hear the wailing then. It is the only way to render abstract history flesh, and must be done.

6

A Valley by the Sea

The policeman from Kardamyla, his motorcycle broken, passes on a donkey. Grandmother Roda, who can neither read nor write, taps her stick up Irini's stairway. She is going to watch the television. Yiorgi, a housing contractor down the street, owns a new Japanese pick-up truck. His neighbour travels by foot or, when the family mule is available, by quadruped. The electric bills here are calculated and printed by computer, but to claim them it is necessary to stand outside the central café where the island postman hollers his list of names. Lagada holds one sure foot in antiquity while another edges cautiously toward the sprinting future. No one here has actually entered the race yet, but many look to be tempted by the inducements. Motor vehicles, for example, are objects of great envy.

Meanwhile, there is still the ancient island quietude. Irini's house stands on a high road overlooking our valley and the sea. Down by the water are clustered most of Lagada's buildings. Behind them stretches the valley floor, folds of silver-green olive trees and emerald green citrus trees enveloping the vegetable warrens beneath, and occasionally a kerchiefed head bobbing mulebound through a golden aperture of light. On the far side of this leafy sweep stands a small white-washed chapel, the dominant symbol of rural Greece, and along from it grows a family of elegant cypress trees, deep green, tall and slender, a clue to the secret order of things. The relentless rockpile hills rise all around. Only this one soft furrow of living green, our valley, has been spared.

From a letter home: 'Here it is enough to wake and move out on to the stoop and feel the sun crisping your skin and the sea and the valley filling your vision, and later to swim at the end of the little harbour where the wind blows wavelets around your eyes and ears and mouth, soothing all your senses and telling you that the simplest pleasures remain the best, and if there is still a need for symbols you can gaze at the ancient fishermen rolling in the bay, following a rhythm older than any inherited memory, a rhythm older than beating blood. So it seems as we float there late in the soft afternoon . . .'

Life is not easy for the people here, but it is not very complicated either. I had forgotten the essential simplicity of each day, forgotten how satisfying is the absence of news media, marketing surveys, junk mail, religious proselytizers, speeding automobiles, joggers, office parties, skin magazines, high fashion, liquor ads and crank phone calls. The manic-depressive face of our industrialized world is not much evident even in Athens, but here in Lagada there is hardly a trace of it. So much is missing from this village, and still we lack for nothing.

Lagada, like most of the island settlements, is too small to support a market of its own. Instead we have the *menaves*, pedlars who travel our coastal road carrying melons, vegetables, fish, milk and bread. Ten years ago they made their way by mule. Now all of them have small trucks, some with loudspeakers. '*Ellate na parete*,' the speakers implore. Come and take. '*Oraia domates, patates, oraia peponia.*' *Oraia peponia*, beautiful melons, are standard fare in the summer. Everything is always *oraia*; even when a vegetable is shrivelled and wormy, no matter, it is *oraia*, though some customers are entitled to their own opinions and usually express them. The *menaves* come every morning, one or two a day, rotating according to an arrangement known only to themselves. The milkman is regular and dependable. He stops three times a week. Some days, when the milk is in short supply, we are rationed to one pint per household, except for those with small children, who are allowed two. Down in the harbour stand three one-room stores patronized according to a complex system of blood ties and family loyalties. They sell cheese, olives, dry goods and wine. As well, two tavernas are operated down there. It is possible never to leave Lagada and still enjoy access to the essential ingredients of Greek life.

Some time has passed since we were last out of the valley. I have forgotten how long, probably no more than a couple of weeks, though it seems like a lifetime, as if memory begins here. Only one road runs in and out of town, and there is little traffic on it. The impression is strong that we are self-sufficient here, living at the centre of the cosmos, indeed that we *are* the cosmos. Enclosed by these hulking rockhills, our valley assumes mythical stature as life's last hope, a final furrow of green stitched in the earth's dry crust. The ancient islanders, dark-eyed sea people who inhabited valleys like this two and three thousand years ago, must have understood their surroundings in much the same way. Larger settlements engaged in trade with other towns, other islands, but small villages like ours would have been occupied with fishing and farming, often without much surplus and therefore without much to exchange. The village existed as the heart of all life, and this centripetal spell was broken only by widespread war or by occasional freebooting pirates, both forces which drove villages further into themselves. This sense of self-containment persists in every island settlement we have come across, and it is a commonplace in

Greece that after the family, the village commands first allegiance.

When I think of the self-centred world view of the Greek villages, I think of Aristarchus of Samos who was probably our first authentic space scientist. Aristarchus, as far as anyone knows, was the first to suggest that the earth revolves around the sun, though Copernicus has been given his laurels. The proposition was remarkable for anyone to develop, but especially for Aristarchus, coming as he did from an archipelago of isolated villages, each certain that the sun served it daily in a kind of grand imitation of the master-slave relationship. Before Greece, before villages, before the polishing of words, man's first formulation beyond himself, I like to think, was that the sun circled the earth. One day it dawned on us, and we basked in the thought. Aristarchus was pitting himself against one of the original eternal verities. It is difficult to imagine what inner resources that must have required. In a sense he had to leave the world behind him – without the protection of a spacesuit.

Despite the origins of scientific thought here, modern science, as we know it in the industrialized world, has taken hold only recently in Greece. This lapse in scientific progress dates back to the European Renaissance, a rea-wakening which did not include the Levant. For centuries the Greek intellect was held captive, first by the closed mind of Byzantium, and then by the closed fist of the Turks. In all that time the great social force here remained the intellectually conservative Orthodox Church. It remains a social force today.

My ancestor dismissed the Greek Church as a 'useless institution', though I should add that he seems to have found Greek monasteries congenial enough. He stayed in them often. I have no way of knowing what formed his anti-clerical judgement. It may have been nothing more than the stock Protestant response to Byzantine ritual and incense. I probably share some of that response myself. Whenever I have been sitting through one of the dark droning services in our village church for more than ten minutes, I am invariably overtaken by the impatient pagan itch to run out and kiss the sun. But to call the Church here a useless institution is historically unfair and a little heartless. Orthodoxy bound the Greeks as a nation through four centuries of Ottoman rule. It still holds families and villages together today, an achievement which seems to us quaint at first glance, but which on reflection looks highly desirable in a world of broken promises and badly bruised hearts. The rigorous discipline imposed on adherents of the Greek Church would doubtless waver in my world to the same degree that all other traditional beliefs have wavered there, but in this village the ancient Christian code continues to offer people a stronghold of religious mystery. Most of the time, I suppose, individual purchase on that mystery is slim, but when a soul needs it, when there is love or birth or death, a union or a parting, sanction and release are close at hand.

We had not been long in Lagada before the bell tolled. It was the second week in July, one day after the onset of a crushing heat wave. Down in the harbour that morning I noticed some paper flyers plastered on trees and lamp posts. They made me wonder vaguely about garage sales and benefit concerts, though I knew the poster had to be in honour of something else. The message looked too solemn for that kind of hucksterism. Outlined in black, it bore a heavily scored heading: KITHEIA. Perhaps the taxman had come from Athens, or the army was giving notice of maneuvers. Later at home I found in the dictionary that KITHEIA means funeral procession. At six o'clock, the heat of the day having lifted slightly, we heard the church bells tolling at the end of our street, and we could see the procession of villagers slithering up the hill like an exhausted old snake about to shed its skin. There was death in the solemn knell, and terror in the drawn eyes of the sobbing widow, and death in the blanched countenance of the corpse planted among dead flowers on an open bier. Even the heat was morbid. The church, close to our house, drew us in. There we lit a candle, as everyone does, for the dead man, and watched the Pappa weave a web of incense around the breathless flesh. This mournful chanting, these anxious candles, must haunt all Greek dreams of death. And how it obsesses them here! The church was overflowing, despite the desperate heat within. The icons of dead saints and then the corpse were kissed, and then again the icons of dead saints; sixteen centuries of death along these walls and one more death that day carried out into the dying sun and slowly up the final climb to the *necrotafeion* where all dead bodies rest.

Black umbrellas glided through our street the next morning as if the skies were still raining deadly misfortune. An old Greek custom for a moment I thought it was, of shielding the head from God's vengeance the day after a passing. They were shields against the sun, of course, because it was said the dead man had succumbed to the heat. But the umbrellas were more than that. Fear of death and a fascination with dying grip these people in a way that recalls the Minoans and Myceneans three and four thousand years ago. Then there was an elaborate death cult with much attention to burial containers, body preparation and grave goods. Now the artifacts are less emphasized. There remain the icons of dead saints and a flickering oil flame above some well-attended graves. Artifacts or no, the death cult flourishes here still. In a few years the man who died of too much sun will be exhumed, his flesh acrumble, his bones to be washed in wine. A year from now in his memory, another ritual will be observed. I was bewildered when the young woman in black, her breast heaving with sorrow, appeared at our door one day, pulled a breadroll out of her basket for me, and moved on down the street. She continued from door to door distributing the bread, in thrall to some painful tie. Her mother, our neighbours explained, had died exactly a year ago, and she was marking her memory with the traditional giving of breadlets.

The Greek Church, to be sure, is not all gloom. The benediction of a new house, the benediction of a sick child, the ceremonies of baptism and marriage, all are acts of hope. We found ourselves walking through a well dressed crowd at the end of our street one Sunday afternoon when we were cheerfully pulled aside and given shot glasses of a fiery pink liqueur. Marcos, the last bachelor of three brothers, was getting married: a happy event, all the participants spilling over with expansive talk and laughter. We followed them into church to witness the intricate Orthodox marriage ritual unfold – paired finger rings and joined head bands, kissing of the icon and of the book, and the endless contrapuntal chanting spiced with waves of thick incense. In the old days, until just after the war, a party was thrown for the newlyweds lasting two or three days. When we ask the older villagers about these parties they smile elusively and murmur *oraia*, happy with their memories of a true wedding feast and a little sad that such feasts will not be repeated. Now the young prefer to spend the weding money on a trip to Athens or one of the fashionable islands like Rhodes.

The village Pappa occupies a position of prestige and authority. If you seek influence, runs an old saying, look to the mayor, the school teacher or the priest. We have not been looking for influence and so have approached none of them, but the Pappa lives on our street in a house beside the church and during the first weeks he would pass our door from time to time and nod gravely. I had the impression he wanted to reach us but did not know where to begin. Once, when I was studying Greek syntax over a beer in the harbour, he peered at my book and murmured approvingly. But he did not speak to us until one evening late in July when we found ourselves at adjoining tables in the harbour café. He turned and asked how our Greek was progressing and we attempted some small talk over a round of drinks. He was, it seemed, assessing our grasp of the language. If verbal communication was going to be too difficult, he would give up on us, however reluctantly. That was what I sensed as he weighed our halting words. Anxious to make a good impression, or perhaps to prove to myself that all those hours of memory work had been justified, I rolled off several simple sentences about the landscape and the weather, waving my arms extravagantly to give the words more meaning. One flying arm did not quite clear an ale glass in its flight path. Across the table top and down on to the Pappa's black caftan slimed the foamy brown. Christ, I thought, I've insulted the priesthood. Unworried, he shrugged and brushed himself off. '*Tipota*,' he said. It's nothing. In Greece a guest, however slightly known, must never be put ill at ease.

The Pappa steered our talk on to his *kiepos*, his garden. Clearly this was a subject close to his heart. Had we tasted the new figs yet? He would take us to his trees and we would pick some. With that we rose and set off in the direction of his land. It struck me that he was accustomed to having people rise and set off when he rose and set off, that the idea of leading people across the land very much appealed to him. He placed his stove pipe hat on his well-made head, greying and thin on top although not yet middle-aged, not yet forty as he would later say, and he strode out on to the hill with an athletic gait, holding himself tall and erect and extending a hand for small children to kiss as we passed. There was a cultivated majesty in the way he progressed, and I sensed that some secret vanity was satisfied by his ability to cut such a noble figure.

We passed our street and the church and continued up the island road until we had cleared the last of the village houses. The floor of the valley rises there, shortening the hills and giving easy access from the road. Over a stone wall the Pappa led us and then down a scruffy trail into the trees. The boundaries of each garden are marked only by memory, partly because local memory is long, and partly because the plots intermingle, a few branches here, a patch of vines there, Stavro's olives overhanging Alexandro's grapes. The fig trees looked to be benevolent creatures, squat and full, with full fat leaves and generous outstretched limbs blessing us as we brushed past.

'Up here,' said the Pappa, 'the gardens are better than below. Here there are no goats, no donkeys, no *copria*, so the gardens are cleaner.' It was indeed a beautiful run of land, pitched high above the town and flanked by the foreshortened hills, but how much the absence of animal shit contributed I could not tell. The Pappa, I later understood, was mildly obsessive about cleanliness.

From tree to tree we went, filling a kerchief and then a small sack with the summer's firstborn figs. One hand plucking high in the branches, and one harnessing his stove pipe hat, Pappa Dimitri looked like a mad hermit trying to touch heaven in a storm. *Oraia sica*, beautiful figs, he chanted, sweet figs, and he peeled two fat ones for us to taste. There were *aprosica*, white figs; *protosica*, early figs; *makriasica*, long-stemmed figs (or literally, faraway figs); and *mavrasica*, black figs. They were all magic, these plump juicy pods, all miraculous. From nothing they came, like desert flowers. There had been no water for weeks. Parched and cracked, the soil should have eaten its young long before. Instead it had cradled them and the pods were swollen with wetness, voluptuous to touch and taste. Desire, and also sadness, begin in a dry garden hung with moist fruit, the sun floating down behind the ragged western hills and radiating a strange unearthly afterglow. We stood in that lavender evening light, the dry air suddenly cool, the miraculous wet fruit hung all about, and we scanned the olive green valley, its pale sky with luminous crescent moon, and wondered why we had not been there always, and had to leave.

Strolling back down the road, I asked the Pappa to come for a glass of wine. 'No, no,' whispered Fay, perhaps foreseeing more spillage, but the Pappa liked the idea, and said he would be right along after washing his hands and depositing his headgear. Once on his own street, he apparently felt free to walk hatless. We brought out our litre of sweet Samian wine purchased from a barrel merchant in Chios Town, and planted chairs on our tiny cement terrace facing the valley and the sea. Pappa Dimitri glided toward us in the failing light, a little bottle of sweet Mavrodaphni in his hand – impossible to offer hospitality to a Greek in his own village. We talked of simple things, the wine, the Greek hills, my part of Canada where there are no valleys by the sea, and we ate and compared a surfeit of figs, piled in bowls at our feet. The stars caught fire, and a solitary bat wheeled around the faint street lamp above us. It was another time when Lagada seemed the omphalos of the planet and the heavens, with plenty of everything and no reason to be anywhere else.

Later, after the Pappa had left and we had eaten our supper of bread, olives, tomatoes and cheese, we walked down toward the presbytery in search of the nocturnal breadman. Lagada being the last village on his delivery route, he usually arrived some time after ten in the evening. The gregarious ones of our street were sitting on a ledge across from the presbytery, and they hailed us as we passed.

Kathieste, kathieste, sit down with us, they said, and they were more insistent than usual, doubtless because they had learned of our fig picking and wanted to hear our impressions. Did we have figs in Canada? Only dried ones? From Greece perhaps? Ah, we would get plenty of figs in Lagada. The season had only just begun. And if we stayed for the olives, we would see that Lagada had the best olives of any village on the island.

The Pappa, who had seen us from his verandah across the street, had ducked down the stairs to his cellar, and now reappeared carrying an enormous bottle, two or three litres, full to the neck with dark liquid. He walked across and presented it to us.

'*To krasi tou Hiou*,' he said. The wine of Chios. We had discussed the island wine earlier on our terrace. It was once, before the European phylloxera epidemic, a prized though highly delicate export commodity. After most of the vines were killed, the reputation and markets were lost, and now only a few peasants continue to press the grapes. But what wine there is, the Pappa assured me, is excellent.

My ancestor offered this comment about Chian wine: 'The island of Scio has been famous from time immemorial for the excellence of its wines. Julius Caesar was very fond of them, for, among his other great qualities, he was a very good judge of wine, which is no doubt the reason why he is so much lauded by certain college and church dignitaries, and proposed by them as a model and example to their pupils; at least I do not recollect any of his other predilections which they could decently think of recommending. The Sciot wine is very delicate and high-flavoured; and it is the more valuable out of the island as the produce is scanty; but chiefly, because it is apt to become putrid in the transportation.' The Roman general's moral stature really had nothing to do with the local wine, but for reasons unknown to us now, John Galt was in an anti-clerical mood again that April day and Julius Caesar provided a useful foil. Galt went on to say: 'The great source of the revenue of the Ottoman state is the tenth of the produce of the land. The oppressive Turks are content with the same proportion of the result of the primary labour of mankind, for the support of their fleets and armies, sultanas and princes, that the meek and lowly priesthood of England require for their backs and bellies.' An interesting and spry comparison this, illustrating the difference in living standards between England and Turkish Greece. The observation was received as a grave insult by some primates of the Anglican Church, and later, when Galt settled in Upper Canada, the local Bishop used the passage against him.

I thought of my ancestor as I sipped the Pappa's gift, smooth yet tangy. It was probably wine very much like this that John Galt tasted when he came to Chios a hundred and seventy years ago. The wine set him thinking about Caesar and the Anglican clergy. It set me thinking about him, and whether I had anything comparable to his clergy about which I wanted to make scathing remarks. Apparently not. A quick search through myself for insults drew a blank. The shallowness of television, the greed of industrial nations, the quacks and charlatans in public life and the professions, the plundering of the ozone layer, none of that, not now please, no. Give me just this glass of wine under starlight with newfound friends, talk and gesture into the warm night on a village street faraway from home, and leave the rest of the world for another day. The world will catch up with us soon enough. There is only one more month for us here at the heart of things, and then we must press on.

Greek life unfolds in groups. We swim in the late afternoon, she and I, floating out in the bay beyond the harbour, all alone in the aquamarine stillness, all alone because the villagers prefer to swim in the late morning just before the noon meal. There is no variation. Always in groups they swim, and always before lunch, every morning. They cannot fathom why we choose solitude near the day's end. Solitude is a shameful condition here, often equated with abandonment. For this reason we can no longer read uninterrupted out on our stoop. Someone is always stopping to rescue us with conversation. A man or woman alone with a book evokes some respect from our neighbours, but also evokes some confusion and pity. Leisure time here is always spent with family and friends. Solitude, though often necessary for work, is generally regarded with distaste.

Lest we insult them, we have tagged along occasionally with the swimmers at noon. Outside the presbytery, at the far end of our street, an impromptu procession begins. The Pappa strikes out in the lead on the half mile walk to a favoured cove. Lagathaki, it is called, after the ravine which climbs up from it. Into his wake are drawn the children and some of the mothers, and from time to time Kosta, the carpenter who lives and works a few doors down from us. The Pappa saves his finely carved wooden staff for these processions, and as he passes our open window I see from my workroom table a neo-Biblical figure swish across the frame: a tall man, a long grey beard, black robes crowned with an elevated black hat, a long white staff firmly gripped and a crowd at his heels.

'*Yiorgo*, Fay,' he calls as he passes, '*tha irthetai?*' Are we coming? And sometimes we do, because it makes them feel better about us, and because during the hot spells a swim in the noonday heat is the only possible thing, and delicious. Most of the villagers either swim off rocks across the bay or off boulders at the mouth of the harbour. The lagathaki is difficult for them to reach. Up on our road, a rarely used accessory route for army vehicles, it is possible to traverse several steep rockpile hills and then descend a shallow gully to the unspoiled cove. Our neighbours are chauvinistically attached to their watering place and refuse to swim anywhere else. They are right; the cove is dazzling in the noon light, clear and clean, its water coloured turquoise and fire blue, but the other pools have their own appeal. A late afternoon immersion at the mouth of the harbour when the houses are still silent, all the afternoon sleepers just rousing themselves for the long evening, the eastern shadows beginning to flow into earthen pools under the pine trees, that too is beautiful.

My wife is the most accomplished swimmer in the village, as if she had been training in northern swimming clubs all her life for this seaside summer. The Greeks, who live by the water, swim badly. I feel right at home. The Pappa and I flounder out, way out, and he insists we go farther and farther, until all the others look like flecks of coloured foam on the waves and I begin to feel like one of those corked bottles floating in mid-ocean with a desperate message inside, the desperate message in my case being that I would like to touch bottom again immediately. Oh well, if we go down, we go down. It would be a memorable place to step off the planet, though the memory would have to be cherished by someone closer to shore.

One day the Pappa and I are out well beyond the arms of the cove, about as far out as my natatory skills will hold me, perhaps farther, when he exclaims, 'Chios is a very old island. Herodotus mentions it in his book.' I see he is surveying the profile of the mountains around the valley, and taking stock of the shoreline. We do not have an unimpeded view of the coast because our valley is set into the island at the foot of a long inlet, but we do get a sense of perspective floating way out here, and it seems to have reminded the Pappa of the grand perspective adopted by Herodotus.

The Father of History, as the Romans called him, is still regarded here with veneration. I venerate him too. He was the first to travel, talk with foreigners and record his findings in prose. There are several mentions of Chios in *The Histories*, mostly brief references of interest only to scholars, but one passage retains a note of irony for anyone visiting the northeast coast today. Opposite Lagada, between Chios and Asia, a thin longish island lies low in the sea. We can spy it slumbering under the Turkish mountains from where we float, out beyond the cove. Oinussai it was originally called, though now often pronounced Ignussai, as if there were a hint of the ignoble there, or so it sounds to anglophone ears. In fact, many Chiots do regard Oinussai with suspicion. Herodotus records that the Chiots refused to sell the little island to the Phocaeans for fear that it would grow into a commercial rival and damage Chian fortunes. This, in an unforeseen way, is what has happened in the twentieth century. Chios has traditionally been a shipowners' island, with generations of inherited wealth and savvy. Seventy-five years ago Lagada was an important fishing port with dozens of seaworthy caiques owned by local captains. Now, gone the days of the wooden hull, there is only one ironrusted old tub festering in the harbour, and an inconsequential string of pleasure boats and small one-man fishing craft. The seamen in Lagada these days ship out with large firms managed from Athens. The irony echoing from Herodotus is that several of these firms are owned by recently established merchants from Oinussai who have parlayed small marine holdings into sizeable fleets, and have thus eaten into Chian supremacy. Fifty years ago Stephano, our landlady's husband, would have owned or worked on a local ship, if not from Lagada then from the larger seagoing village of Kardamyla or from Chios town. Now he is the steward for a freighter owned in Oinussai. The Chiots regard their rivals across the water not as parvenus, with the snobbery that connotes, but simply as shrewd comers who have stolen a march on them. Rivalry and mistrust run rampant in these islands. Snobbery is an uncommon trait exhibited mostly by those who have been educated abroad.

The Pappa asks me this day if I will swim to the island with him. As the island lies several miles away, I decline. 'No, no,' he persists, 'not to Oinussai. We will swim to the little island,' and he waves to a clump of brush and stunted trees on a seabound rock hundreds of yards away and equally out of reach. I tell him I will watch him, certain that if he goes I will watch him drown. He relents. Would we come for lunch then? This strikes me as a better idea, safer and more interesting.

We have eaten with his family often since the day he picked us figs. The Pappa likes our company, partly because we are in his eyes educated people. He too is schooled, one of the relatively few learned Pappas. The vast majority of Orthodox village priests learn their liturgy by rote and have at most a grade school education. Little more than a quarter have completed the Greek equivalent of high school and then studied in a seminary. These educated Pappas can read the ancient classical texts and speak and write katharevousa, a formal version of modern Greek. Katharevousa was outlawed in 1977, after a century of wrangling over its usefulness. When it was first developed by the expatriate intellectual Adamantios

Korais (whose father was a Chiot and after whom the Chios library is named) in the eighteenth century, katharevousa served as a rallying point for nascent Greek nationalism, but the artificial nature of a language frozen in writing, immured to rejuvenation, soon spelled its fall from grace. Stilted and overelaborate, used only by the well educated and the well employed, katharevousa became a source of social tension and, from time to time, political upheaval. The riots which erupted in the streets of Athens in 1901 over publication of the New Testament in demotic, the common living language, gave evidence of strong feelings on both sides of the issue. Katharevousa was and still is defended by conservative elements, while demotic has been championed by liberals. The Church is exempt from the 1977 law, Orthodox liturgy being cast in a variation of katharevousa and still permitted.

The Pappa thinks it a pity that formal language has been officially renounced. I have my own ideas, but keep them to myself. Foreigners, especially those who speak Greek imperfectly, may not easily interfere. In any case, my feelings have been uttered eloquently by two of the best modern Greek writers, the novelist Kazantzakis and the poet Seferis. Both wrote their remarkable works in demotic.

Although there is a yawning cultural gap between us, Pappa Dimitri and I pass the time together amicably. He is interested in the outside world, and since a Greek priest is not permitted to travel beyond his country's borders without dispensation from the ecclesiastical authorities, I provide a rare link for him. Despite their voyages as sailors, most of the local men know the outside only superficially. The world appears to them as a vast stretch of salt water broken occasionally by cargo wharves and harbour shanties tucked under plate-glass skylines. Port life they know about, but little else.

Around Pappa's table we talk of the differences between our country and Greece, our lives and theirs. Weeks ago, he and the Pappathia, his wife, put to us what would have seemed anywhere else an array of intimate questions: how much money we made, how much we paid for our house in Canada, when we planned to have children, what were our religious beliefs, and so on. All these probes darted out one after another the night we first sat outside with our neighbours opposite the presbytery. To the Greeks there is nothing unseemly or prying about such enquiries. They make them of every newcomer, and I think their free curiosity, the refreshing lack of pretence, must endear them to all but the most pompous foreigners.

These basic questions have long since been answered, the Pappa and his family are sure of us and we can discuss whatever we wish, though in practice we spend much of the time talking about food. Like most Greeks we have met, this family approaches food as a topic of endless fascination. They want to know if we think Greek food is expensive and if we think Greek cooking is good. They want to know what we put on our table at home and how it compares to what they put on theirs. We spend many contented hours here without straying far from our stomachs, and the Pappathia's excellent fare goes a long way to justify our single-mindedness.

Still, even with the ease of conversation, it is bizarre to be sitting in a room darkened to stay the heat, with an Orthodox priest, his wife and daughter and son, speaking an old language of unfamiliar cadence and form, a language we have barely begun to handle. Despite some awkward pauses we do manage to flush out most essential meanings with our hands and the dictionary at my elbow. But there are moments when the situation seems quite unreal, as if someone else had imagined it and planted us here for dramatic or satirical purposes. Like Gulliver we are, or like Pantagruel, charged by a whim of fate to see afresh with innocent eyes this revealing corner of the globe. No one but an infant or a fool possesses innocent eyes. The exhilarating thing is that we are naturally a little of both here, both child and fool, because we see some things as if we were just beginning, as if our world were just taking shape, and because we have some of a fool's freedom from responsibility. This is not our land. We are witnesses here, nothing more.

For a northerner in Greece, one of the most striking discoveries is the division between the sexes. The cafés are frequented by men, and from time to time a couple will stop for a drink, but never an unaccompanied female. The Pappathia, when we come for lunch, rarely sits down with us until half way through the meal and then often occupies only a humble corner of the table. She and her daughter serve the men and guests as a matter of course. The Pappa jokes that he cannot boil an egg and has no wish to learn. His work is out of the house, he explains, and the Pappathia's within. Roles are rigidly observed in Lagada. Irini, our landlady, showed discomfort when we invited her down to the harbour one evening for a drink. She declined mysteriously, then several days later confessed that it was thought improper for wives of absent seamen to be seen enjoying themselves in a public establishment. Marriages are still arranged here, and dowries are still an important part of the pact.

The division of roles was brought home to me, literally, one morning when Irini and Fay were off together in Chios Town. Irini's mother was upstairs for the day looking after her two grandsons. At eleven o'clock she appeared in my doorway with a plate of hot food. More unbelievable Greek hospitality, I thought with embarrassment, taking this to be another of the many undeserved offerings of raw and cooked food we had been receiving from our neighbours. Then I realized what she was saying.

'Your wife is not here. You will have no lunch.' A man without a woman in Greece is in danger of starvation. My wife gone for the day, Irini's mother was afraid I would be unable to find any food.

For a while I thought I had made a big mistake. I should have come to live here years earlier and married a woman from this village. Then I remembered what the men here do for a living. They work for months at a time, sometimes for a year or longer without a break, in the bowels of hot stinking ships which plow across vast wet deserts of boredom, night after day after night after day in the same tiny cabin far away from wives and children. It is easy to bemoan the lot of women here. Using our wholly inapplicable standards, one arrives at a meaningless judgement. Outside of the small elite, their men are not to be envied. We have met Europeans and North Americans who gripe over the enslavement of the Greek female. A misplaced litany this is, borrowed from their cultures at home. In Athens there is some evidence of womanly restiveness, understandable in that different setting. Here we see none.

Still, I will stick my neck out and decry the Greek custom of chaining females to ceaseless mourning. I know its history and its apparent logic, that the men, breadwinners and power-brokers, deserve to believe they will be missed, but I cannot accept it. Our neighbour is twenty-six, a pretty young woman in the prime of life. She will dress in black for the rest of her years. Her husband was asphyxiated in the hold of a ship when she was twenty-five. In many ways her life is finished. Only an unlikely rematch can save her from years of gloomy resignation. I see no redemption for anyone in this clinging to the dead, only misery and doom and death itself. But we offer such opinions primarily to salve some uneasiness in our own hearts. Nothing I say will ever help the sad young widow.

For the rest, who but a Greek can praise or condemn the arrangement of roles here? The women love my wife, are fascinated by her, partly because she travels and they do not, but we see no sign of envy, no resentment of their own womanhood. When I remember the Pappathia solemnly serving us at her husband's command the first time we ate with them, the surprise and twinge of dismay we felt, I remember also the picture of the Pappa and Pappathia sitting outside the presbytery on a hot July night, their hands entwined like young lovers' hands and their faces at peace. Let us accept love where we find it, and hold the naysaying for our own hard losses.

Since we first visited his house, the Pappa's sixteen-year-old son Stamatis has worked at preparing us for the big August party. From time to time we have seen dancing in the harbour tavernas. These have been small private affairs, someone engaging a musician or two for a family party. There is nothing like the plaintive wail of bouzouki filtering up the hillside in darkness, pulling one gently out of bed and into the moonlit street with a cocked ear, and then inveigling one down the hill to an onlooker's table, the better to listen and watch. Ah yes, says Stamatis, but they are *little* parties. We must come down to the tavernas when all the villagers will celebrate the night of August fifteenth. There we will see dancing and hear music such as we have never before encountered. Stamatis reminds us every few days of the coming event, and has given us impromptu lessons in the simpler of the Greek dances. August fifteenth is not the village saint's day, which falls in September, but Lagadans traditionally reserve a night in high summer for a fund-raising party to benefit the village coffers. August is the month when the largest number of relatives are visiting from Athens and abroad, and the feast gives the reconstituted village a chance to reaffirm its faith in itself.

August fifteenth. Stamatis takes us down to the harbour and places us at a table, always the gestures of hospitality here. The harbour is full to bursting with provender, music, people and their merriment. Enormous quantities of food and drink are being consumed. Just when all the participants at a table seem to loll into final lethargy, one of them will order another battery of meatballs, squid, potatoes and cheese, and everyone will begin again. It is quite incredible to see the volume of food disappearing here. We make the naïve error of moving to sit at another neighbour's table for the second half of the evening. They are positioned at the edge of the dance floor and the view is superior, but they insist we eat and drink as if the evening had just begun. If not, they will feel inadequate as hosts. So we do eat and drink again, enough for several days it seems.

Everyone is here, the faces we have seen only vaguely through fences and windows, the nodding acquaintances, the neighbours and the friends. Mike the grocer is here, a former seaman who spent some time in Montreal. He has helped us with the language and with introductions, and we have joined those loyal to his store. We raise glasses now across the sea of tables. Old Ianni, the butcher's brother, who likes to buy us a drink from time to time, sits on the outskirts of the crowd and winks when he sees us dance. Back from travels on Rhodes are Marco and his new bride. We are seated at their table now, along with Marco's two brothers, Ianni and Yiorgi and their wives. Marco continues to clink his glass to mine, expressing endless delight that we were at his wedding, his enthusiasm stretching wildly like an overblown balloon. And finally Marco does pop, sinking down on to the table, an absolute deadweight despite much discreet coaxing by his two brothers. *Stin yassas*, Marco. I drink to you.

The dances, as Stamatis has shown us, are either Greek or Turkish, and any good island stepper knows the difference. The most obviously Turkish patterns are homosexual. As Byron bluntly put it, the Turk is given to buggery. Whether that remains true I don't know, but if these traditional dances are any indication, it must have been true in the past. The men shimmy and shake for one another, striking lewd and suggestive postures which advertise intended sodomy later behind closed doors, or at least are meant to leave that impression. If they are good ham actors, the men elicit applause from the crowd. That these dances are still performed is not surprising. Friendship here between unpromised young men and women are at best tense and inhibited and more often non-existent. The villagers prefer to see two boys or a brother and sister dance together than to see an unaffiliated boy and girl who simply like each other.

More interesting is to watch two women dance. They are moving slowly now, radiating womanly rhythms into the crowd, into the harbour, into the night. A black-haired beauty from Athens has touched my wife's arm and invited her on to the floor. This too is a Turkish dance calling for the lithe shoulder-shimmy, and Seta, my wife's Athenian beauty, ripples off the music with maddening grace. Her limbs caress the music as if it were a lover. The dancing here is sensually explicit on all sides, and I see now that it is their release, for the young like Seta a release from celibacy, and for the older ones a release from closely guarded marriages and channeled desire. Greek island men and women rarely touch in public. Tonight sexual concealment is lifted and the blood begins to find its natural course.

Toward dawn it is, a far-fetched and inexact hour

somewhere between inspiration and delirium, when a fat little man prances toward us, stops to steady himself against the huge eucalyptus tree, places a full bottle of wine on his head, and lurches on to the dance floor. The bottle attaches itself to his skull miraculously. I think he must have been born with it. Yes, the little fat man definitely had a wine bottle for a placenta. This would also explain his unusual shape. How else could he dance as he does, kicking his feet and slapping palm to heel without the bottle slipping? An amazing performance the man with the glass afterbirth gives us. He seems a little desperate, as if this is his secret vocation and he can practise it only once a year, twelve months of dancing to work into a mere pinch of time on this wine-soaked night, but he does it, the whole year's worth, and then kicks a toe high in the air and releases his birthright which sails away, applauding him with a crash as it lands, until it is needed again next year.

Two men are helping Marco into a car. The music has died. At the top of the hill there is an empty bed for us. The black sky gives a little, leaking a faint spray of mauve.

In August we receive another telephone call. It is Mr Argenti again, on the island for a few weeks and throwing a party at his estate in the Kampos. We are invited.

The bus takes us to Chios Town in the afternoon and there we stroll through thinly peopled streets, most shops having closed at one for the day. Only the cafés and tavernas remain open, and a handful of scrounging merchants. Along the harbour the evening *volta* beings, a ritual promenade which fills the waterfront from sundown to eleven. This is the fashionable place to be. In the smaller, humbler eateries hidden on streets behind the harbour, groups of unshaven men are hunched together for the night's heavy drinking.

We board another bus in the plateia, this one bound for the village of Thimiana in the Kampos. We know where to debark, because we have been here once before, though never in the dark. The driver tells us when we have reached our crossroads and lets us out into the tar-black night. The moon has not yet risen or hides behind a bank of clouds. In this district only those houses willing to pay for their own street lamps have light. Our matches lead us halfway down the lane and then we are blind. I remember Katy complaining that there was a plague of rats around here. These smooth coils my hand brushes as we grope along someone's wall, are they vines or rodents' tails? Outside Katy's house there is a glimmer of light, so we stop to say hello, then continue down the road to the Argenti compound. Cars crowd the area around the ducal blue doors. Apparently we are the only ones to arrive on foot.

Across the tessellated pebble floor of the entrance way and through the ducal doors we go. What we see is much the same as what J. L. Stephens saw when he visited a partly ruined Chian mansion in 1839: 'We entered through the large stone gateway into the courtyard beautifully paved in mosaic in the form of a star, with small black and white stones. On our left was a large stone reservoir perhaps twenty-five feet square, still so perfect as to hold water, with an arbour over it supported by marble columns; a venerable grapevine completely covered the arbour. The garden covered an extent of about four acres, filled with orange, lemon, almond and fig trees; overrun with weeds, roses and flowers, growing together in wild confusion.' The black and white pebble floor is here, and so is the reservoir. John Galt admired the large garden wheels used on Chios to raise water up from the depths to grade-level pools. The Argentis have one of these, brightly painted and still functional. Beyond the water wheel and beyond the wide terrace lie the citrus trees and tangled flower beds we visited a month ago, and somewhere beyond these is hidden P. P. Argenti's restored Chian villa.

Pandely Argenti's mother has come from England, and some friends are visiting from Italy. The librarians are here, and Elefteros the meteorologist, and there are several Chiots from the shipowning class. Two fiddles and an accordion serenade us, cut flowers blush everywhere against pale marble columns, and the terrace gleams with squares of fresh white linen smoothed across a dozen tables set for four. I'm not sure about this scene. Suggestive of an English peer's garden party, it also echoes something less straightforward, a film about Italian wealth and decadence perhaps, or the early work of Salvador Dali. Underneath these faultless tablecloths, I would not be surprised to find someone's chauffeur mounting a maid, or one of Dali's disembodied hands caressing the Contessa's velvet gown. If there is not a Contessa in this crowd, there ought to be.

We are introduced to the aged matriarch who is holding court beside a marble column adorned with several bushels of bright cut flowers. I present our meagre nosegay of carnations.

'How sweet of you,' she says sadly, but I do believe she means it. Perhaps having to acknowledge so many dead blooms is a melancholy task. My flowers disappear forever into the severed jungle at her side, making no difference. I appreciate their predicament. Already I feel a little lost here myself.

My wife has been led off to meet one of the Italians. Pandely introduces me to a shipowner and we talk awhile. In his thirties, about my age, he lives in London and takes the summer holiday on his native island. Someone has told him that I am writing a guide-book to Chios, and he congratulates me on my undertaking. As there are few tourists on this island, and therefore few buyers for such a book, he must imagine me to be either very wealthy or very dim-witted. At a double table for eight Mr Argenti seats my wife and me. Our plates are filled with Greek and Italian delicacies, our glasses charged with wine, our ears lulled by island music, our eyes stilled with blooms. It is all an elegant massage of the senses, and we enjoy it, yes we do, though the insouciance is a little cloying, the polish a little rich. There is no naked chauffeur under the table after all, and if there were, no one here would give him more than half a wink. These eyes have seen all they wish to see. They have gone past hunger in favour of disdain. One must lightly amuse and, above all, deliver words silkily, allowing the forced illusion of a well oiled world to attain high levels of perfection. That is all that must be done here. The rest has been forgotten.

Several languages are on parade. Greek and some English take hold at the other tables, but we are using Italian, a medium which gives me a lot of time for introspection and social analysis. I don't speak a word of it. There must be a way for us to break into this Roman group. I am thinking idly of all the European revolutions since 1789, not a good starting point for clever conversation here, so I ask the self-assured woman across from me whether she speaks any Greek. She eyes me coldly.

'But I *am* Greek,' she replies, and then lists her languages, six of them, though she discounts German because it hurts her throat. That said, she turns away. I have squeezed in a few words of French.

The middle-aged couple beside us turn to talk. Because she is Belgian their domestic language is French. He is a Chiot, though spends little time here. They have lived in Egypt, and in northern Europe, globe-trotters but not jet-setters, not at all attached to the fast glittering life. Soft, gentle folk they are, and we warm to them easily. An amateur botanist and ornithologist, he passes each day in his garden and describes to me now its many virtues. Would we like to visit them one day at their house in Chios Town? Yes indeed. It would be an entertainment to watch the landowner tend his exotic birds.

Dinner wanes and the tables are shifted to make room for dancing. Dimitri the librarian and his baritone friend belt out a brace of songs, and then the champagne arrives and everybody sings and we dance an easy three-step, the *hasaposerviko*. Tonight's music, Pandely tells us, is all of Chian origin. A little later he pauses by my chair and asks why I am still sober.

'Canadians are supposed to get drunk,' he says, faintly miffed. I am reminded of the child who saw a stripeless zebra in his storybook. What to do? I haven't the heart to get drunk here tonight. I think a drunken Canadian, like the naked chauffeur, would induce only boredom in this crowd. My chicken imitation, for example, I'm sure would go nowhere here. There are one or two other unnatural acts I could perform to liven things up, but as we have to renew our Greek visas soon, it is probably best to continue cultivating the reputation of innocent bystander.

A candlelit procession descends the stairway of the gatehouse. At the heart of the procession moves Pandely Argenti. He is moving slowly and gravely through the flickering shadows. He is bringing us dessert. In his gentle embrace floats an enormous baked Alaska pie. Today is Pandely's name day. He is marking it with the party, but more particularly with the pie. Someone proposes another toast, and then we eat the ceremonial meringues.

Time to go. The landowner and his Belgian wife have offered us a lift in their cab. We say our good-byes softly. This is the moment when my wife and I should be throwing champagne bottles in the air and singing a pornographic version of our national anthem, but we are not drunken Canadians tonight. We take leave of the haute international bourgeoisie as they take leave of each other, with murmured adieus and harmless little bows. How sad not to be a drunken Canadian just when one is needed. And to think that I have so often squandered my talents for the role at home where they were least appreciated.

The landowner transports us into Chios Town, then instructs the driver to see us to our village and send him the bill. Greek hospitality knows no bounds, whether in the village or in the gardens of the rich. I can't think of anywhere I would rather be.

We do stop to see the landowner and his wife one day. They give us lemon squash on the terrace, then show us around their vast acreage, all the more impressive for lying right in the heart of Chios Town. The property has resisted all pressures for development and remains not so much a large garden as a small farm amid concrete block apartment buildings and the humming retail district.

As we begin, the landowner and I discover to our mutual satisfaction that we are both mild hypochondriacs. He solemnly recites a list of recently identified diseases on the island: Maltese fever in the milk, infections from leakages in the town waste main, dangerous microbes carried by the local dog population, and a potent strain of influenza. We are both suitably repelled by this catalogue, though our wives look on mockingly. Maltese fever being a potentially fatal illness, I enquire whether he is still drinking the milk. Yes, the vats in the dairy have been sterilized and the cows are clean.

Our alliance against disease seems to put the landowner in good spirits for a tour of the grounds. He points with pride to his pink hibiscus, to the giant palms he has imported from Africa, to his oleander and laurel bushes, and to his baby lime trees now bearing little fruitlets. We see a family of goats, a garden of gargantuan summer squash, and row upon row of swelling mandarins. Here and there still stand a few senile mulberry trees, relics from the days when the island was envied for its finely wrought silks. And the ancient Chian water wheel has survived. Once turned by mule-power, it has been mechanized and now feeds a system of aqueducts watering the land.

Past the family chapel where the landowner's forebears lie, we come to his birds. Cockatoos, quail and parakeets splash an array of eerie colour as they bob behind the grey skein of their cages. More striking still are the multi-coloured Chinese pheasants, their phantasmagoric plumage punctuated by beady blood-sucking eyes.

'That one,' says the landowner pointing, 'is mad.' I can believe it. He is beautifully feathered, arrogant, withdrawn and evidently murderous. How could it be otherwise? The landowner, who breeds the birds, opines with a shrug that he must have made a mistake with this one. Perhaps. But the Descendents of Paradise appear in many guises.

As we leave the birdhouses, our host waves up at one of the stark apartment towers shadowing his land.

'C'est terrible,' he laments, a feeling anyone could easily share once inside this magic preserve. Yes, all the world should be a perfumed garden teeming with orchids and African palms. Instead it is teeming with people, each needing a place to live. I am one of them. The landowner cuts a sad, impossible figure when he bemoans the spread of concrete, as if he were one of his own ancestors risen from below the family chapel, shouting into another century insults we no longer understand.

The Belgian wife gives us two delicate little quail eggs

and a handful of limes. They walk us down to the garden gate, good people from another epoch. Out in the street, the shops are still bustling. It is not quite noon. This is the *Aplotarias*, the Street of the Hanging Silks, now the principal shopping street. In the days of high prosperity here, the way was lined with fabric merchants, their wares hung out on view. Nowadays a vast assortment of goods changes hands in this street: fruit from the peasants' carts, souvlaki from small smoking windows in the side lanes, tobacco at the kiosks, clothing and household supplies in crowded cubby-holes and also in more expensive display rooms. The character of the shops has changed, but the jostle and confusion of a busy shopping street in the Levant is probably much as it was centuries ago. I am certain my ancestor walked this way to see the hanging silks, and I think of him now poking through the doorways of these buildings to examine the wares of the accomplished Chian weavers. I can see him quite clearly here. The landowner may think he needs his garden oasis to maintain a lifeline to the past. If so, he is wrong. Lifelines to the past can be woven and kept within.

The Pappa has invited us to Sikiada, his native village. He owns a plot of land there on which he has built a house with his own hands. It will probably form the major part of his daughter's dowry, unless the progressive elements in Greece have their way and the dowry custom is outlawed. If not part of her marriage agreement, the house will be his to use in retirement.

Bring a sack, he tells me. We are going to pick tomatoes in another one of his gardens. Sikiada is derived from the Greek word *siko*, meaning fig, so we might also find some sweet fruit. If we do, it will probably taste the same as the fruit picked around our village. Sikiada is only a couple of miles away, though the twisting coastal road makes the distance longer.

The Pappa insists on paying our fare. We board an old machine outside the church gates, descend the hill and pass through our little valley whose floor is only a couple of hundred yards wide. Then slowly up the opposite slope we go and across a rocky saddle, twisting and grinding, until we can see Pantoukios. Built directly below a steep rockhill, this fairy-tale village sits at the snug end of a long loop of water. It looks to house about a dozen inhabitants, and a splash of green proves they grow something down there. Some painted boats bob off the tiny wharf. But in truth, Pantoukios is not really a village at all. It is the fishing port which serves Sikiada, a much larger settlement in the hills behind. Until the advent of fast overland transport, each was dependent on the other. Now the attachment is mostly nominal, though still strongly felt. As the bus turns away from the sea, the Pappa points below and says he used to clamber down these hills as a child and swim there. Pantoukios and Sikiada, he says, have always been *mazi*, together.

The bus stops beside Sikiada's main café. We are unable to see the water now. This village was established when there were still pirates abroad, some say two hundred years ago, some say a little later. None of the buildings are visible from the sea. Marauders, so the theory went, would plunder only the tiny port, and then sail on.

The Pappa leads us on a tour. Not far from the café, he sees his grandmother, hard of hearing and toothless, infirmities which can be expected at the age of a hundred and two. He calls to her and she scrambles over to him, kneels and kisses his hand. Then he sits her in a chair and has us take their picture. We pass his poor uncle, a pastry pedlar wandering the late afternoon streets with a tray of little cakes. Old Elias, the hard drinking man who finds odd jobs in Lagada, nods and winks as we walk by his door. Everyone here knows the Pappa and greets him amicably.

He shows us the tiny two-room dwelling where he was born, and the place just like it where the Pappathia came into the world, and then we continue down the narrow street past more of these low crouching abodes, all neatly whitewashed, to his sister's door. There we stop to drink cherry juice and talk in the shade. Her husband is away, first mate on a freighter sailing the Great Lakes. As we leave, the Pappa's niece offers us each a lemon blossom, sacrificing two precious lemons later in the year.

On the next street over his aunt sits in eucalyptus shade, a bucket of fresh almonds between her knees. She offers us handfuls, and we break their skins on the rocks underfoot. Our stroll through this village is dream-like, as if we had stepped into a sprawling unroofed mansion where time runs fluidly in every direction. The generations stretch easily back and forward here, the Pappa's grandmother passing her great-grandchildren in the lane, aunts and uncles living one street over, siblings or children next door. The long history of a family collects itself in the bystreets, reaffirmed daily by touchable flesh. In my world the bloodline assembles mostly in letters and night thoughts, a faraway and mysterious thing, a liberation and a loss. Here in the hot months, the village is one enormous domicile, the street both corridor and kitchen, everyone living within earshot and eyeshot of family and friends, everyone watchful and jostling, caring and critical, as in a complex dream.

To the Pappa's new house we descend, away from the infinite family. His land, a new plot, is situated on the outskirts of town. Here he sheds his cassock and we harvest tomatoes, putting aside small ones for the winter *kremasma*, the drying of strung fruit, and throwing together a worm-eaten pile for the goat. House-proud, the Pappa pauses to tell us how he laid the foundation and built the walls, section by section, several years' work, and how fine a view his verandah will command. He comes two or three times a week, he says, sometimes with the Pappathia, and occasionally they stay the night. I sense a pleasure in him never before evident and realize now that they are both uneasy exiles beyond the separating hills, even though Legada sits less than half an hour down the coastal road. Their hearts will remain in their native settlement, and they will continue to make regular pilgrimages here as long as they are able. Whether in Australia or just around the next bend in the shoreline, a Greek outside his village is never quite at home.

7

The Silence of Pythagoras

Evening, and all light angles down behind the rocky furrow where our valley disappears into the hills. A shadow creeps slowly across the olive-laden kampos, and continues up the opposite slope until only a small luminous oval crowns its stony pate. Once the children are called to bed, silence falls, and then are loosed the sounds of the dark. We lie and listen to the yelping dogs answer their own echoes from the hills, and when they tire, we listen to the forlorn single-noted owl who haunts this vale at midnight. Occasionally, when least expected, we are startled by the tortured scream of a lacrimose ass calling down the millenia of mammalian evolution, pleading helplessly for a better voice. Hee-haw. Hee-hee-hee-hee-haw. What a sad inheritance.

In the morning we test the weather by listening for the choral cicadas. If they begin before eight, we know the day will be scorchingly hot. By nine at the latest they are always squeaking their high-pitched warble, a sound made by scraping the wings, or so we are told. I have my own ideas about this constant buzz, a call which strikes me as too unearthly to originate anywhere in the animal kingdom. There is in Chian folklore a tradition of local hobgoblins, *kallikantzaroi* by name, the deformed spirits of those born the week following Christmas. They were said to walk village streets at night and harass ordinary folk, but I am sure they no longer do. I walk the dark streets myself every evening and have never felt their presence. No, they have joined the little people who live in the ether above us. For amusement they all keep busy skipping tiny pebble discs across the sunny pool suspended over our heads. It is the sound of these hundreds of pebbles darting across smooth water that we hear on a hot island morning and ascribe to cicada wings.

Ample time for idle speculation here; and why not indulge in it? We are a long way from the anxieties of men making their mark, making their fortunes, making their bloody mistakes. The monkish life is not for me, but some days of tranquil thinking are always welcome. I have been able to resurrect Pythagoras on a lonely rock by the water here, and to discover some good reasons for his persistent appeal.

Pythagoras has been called the father of philosophy. There were others before him, notably Thales and Anixamander, but it is Pythagoras whose formative thought endured as an influence, and often as a puzzle, for centuries after his death, and some of whose premises acted as guideposts for Artistotle and Plato. He was an extraordinary man, leaving pivotal contributions to philosophy, music and mathematics. He was also a deeply religious man with complex beliefs on the universe and the soul. He stands at the beginning of rational thought, but is unique among the great Greek thinkers in having moved back and forth easily between the pre-rational magic world of superstition and taboo, and the world of rigorous logic represented by mathematics. In fact, the division of intellectual expression into the categories of rational and irrational thought would probably have seemed false to Pythagoras, alien to his belief in the essential unity of all things.

I say 'probably' because we can never know for certain in what precise terms the philosopher couched his beliefs. None of his writings survive, and the long tradition which followed him, close to a thousand years, has muddied the record. Still, a consensus does exist among most scholars that Pythagoras himself was probably responsible for certain salient aspects of the cult which surrounded his memory, and that he probably did make the important mathematical and musical discoveries for which he was subsequently revered. It is unlikely that he possessed a golden thigh, as some of the later Pythagoreans claimed, but his intellect certainly glittered, and shines on us still. In a curious way, he is the philosopher of our own age, or ought to be. I make no claims for myself as a philosophical elucidator; here I want only to venture some simple notes about his accomplishments and beliefs. These islands whisper his name, and give the unbroken quiet and solitude necessary to raise his ghost. At home, with the world crashing in on all sides, the remote pursuits of philosophy often seem a fool's errand. Here they are more credible.

Pythagoras was born on Samos about 570 B.C., a century before the golden age of classical Greece. His father is thought to have been a gem-engraver, and it is likely that the son would have been trained in that same craft. Samos was approaching an unparalleled age of prosperity and would reach the apex of its power around 538 under the tyrant Polycrates. Pythagoras' fascination with numbers may have been fed by the unusually brisk commerce enjoyed by Samian craftsmen and traders in his early years. As he grew older, however, revulsion apparently set in, possibly at the excesses of the pirate king, and around 530 B.C. he emigrated to Croton, a leading Greek colony in southern Italy. He died there around the turn of the century. Little more is known of his life, though many embellishments were applied to these scant facts by later generations of admirers.

Apart from his famous geometric theorem, Pythagoras is also credited with the discovery of the numerical ratios which determine the concordant scale. He was our first musicologist. The octave, fifth and fourth, regarded as primary intervals, were discovered to depend on fixed ratios: one to two, three to two, and four to three. This was probably revealed to him through investigations on the *kanon*, a simple one-stringed instrument with a moveable bridge. The rate of vibration of a string being inversely proportional to its length, if one string is twice as long as another, it will vibrate at half the speed and produce the interval of an octave. If only half again as long, it will produce the interval of a fifth, and so on. With the right intuition and careful experiments on a pair of single-stringed *kanons*, a patient man could establish the ratios. In this way, we speculate, the mysteries of melodic progression were plucked open by Pythagoras. Harmony, as we know it today, was not developed until later, though the word *armonia* was used to describe what the Pythagoreans believed were similar fixed ratios among the heavenly bodies, which they claimed sent out a sort of astral hymn. No one, as far as we can tell, ever heard this galactic melodic progression, but the idea remained a catchy one. Certain Renaissance poets took it up when they peppered their poems with the Pythagorean slogan, the Harmony of the Spheres.

Probably as a result of these musical discoveries, and because of the uncanny properties of the right-angled triangle, the Pythagoreans endowed numbers with mystical power. The number ten was thought to be a perfect thing. Its perfection can be partly explained by the four integers involved in the musical ratios: one, two, three and four, which make its sum. Here we step back into the world of magic. The number four was equated with justice, five with marriage, and so on. Not mere symbols these numbers were. Four *was* justice, perhaps in somewhat the same sense as thirteen, for some people, *is* disaster. Numbers were considered somehow to have substance. Through them a divine order was imposed on the world, invisible to the eye but discernible by the mind.

Above all, Pythagoras was a metaphysician and moralist. His view of the soul probably stems from, or was encouraged by, his sense of the unseen mathematical Principle. The essence of every creature, the soul too was unseen, an invisible wisp on the wheel of transmigration. The body was the temporary dwelling place of the soul, and the soul was doomed to continue hunting for similar apartments through all eternity unless it was fortunate and inhabited for one lifetime a human being sufficiently withdrawn to have lived all his hours purely and nobly, in which case the single soul might escape the body altogether and rejoin the universal and divine soul drifting in the ether, lulled, doubtless, by the harmony of the spheres. The doctrine of reincarnation aside, it is clear that strains of Pythagoreanism later found their way into the teachings of Christianity.

In order to favour the tenant soul, its temporary landlord was admonished by Pythagoras to live the good life. We descend into the realm of magic again. According to Pythagorean tradition, the good life included touching the earth when it thundered, spitting on one's nail pairings, keeping swallows out of the house, leaving on the floor what had fallen from the table, and not eating beans, to mention only a few of his curious commands. Today we are tempted to ask why a little bird–shit was considered inappropriate when there were already bits of food and finger nails littering the floor, but our irreverent impulse misses the point. The undercurrent running through all of Pythagorean thought is just the opposite of irreverence: heartfelt awe. Sometimes, as can happen with awe, the mood turned to terror.

Here is the list of ten opposites, or opposing principles,

said to have been drawn up by Pythagoras and his disciples:

unlimited	limit
even	odd
plurality	one
left	right
female	male
moving	at rest
crooked	straight
darkness	light
bad	good
oblong	square

Fear is creeping into the words now, fear of the over-whelming, fear of the unknown, fear of women (over-whelming, unknowable), fear of chaos. There lurks an obsessive dread in the lefthand column. On the right lie self-control and safety. This dread is the terrible quid pro quo paid for an uncensored entanglement with the irra-tional. The world was teeming with masks and mysterious malign forces. Pythagoras came to terms with them, not as we have done, using science and a token dash of religious sentiment, but by conceiving of man himself as a mask, another mystery. There are many differences between the Pythagoreans and industrial man. Great tomes have been written examining some of them, and much more could be said, but surely the simplest and most poignant difference is that Pythagoras was bound without reserve to the planet. He was a creature among his fellow creatures, a being in tune with all time, whereas we, since the beginning of science, have set ourselves apart. We are the aloof observers, and also bugs speared on a pin, also the helpless specimens.

Logical thought we control and manipulate. The irra-tional, the gothic, the surrealistic, these modes have a mind of their own, potent and sometimes dangerous, a mind which writes automatically, has nightmares, hallucinates, invents chilling tales, tells outlandish jokes, paints strange symbols and can kill in a rage. Most of us accord this mind benign neglect, though some cultivate it in an intensely controlled setting, on the analyst's couch or through an art form. Some few still yield it to religious passion, but by and large our rational, industrial world is suspicious of this spooky mind and holds it at bay, except where it can be packaged for sale – as therapy or as folklore or as marketable art. Pythagoras and his circle feared and then coopted the mysteries of the world, engaging them in a system of tenet and taboo. Our industrial civilization has dealt with these fears through science, which explains many of them away, but in so doing we have diminished or denied outright that part of the psyche which allows access to such fearsome mystery. We have charted a hundred and three elements, but have also, to put it boldly, lost our minds.

This loss began with Aristotle, the first great observational scientist. He was an important amateur lawyer, anthropologist, meteorologist, psychologist, drama critic and more than an amateur biologist and logician. Here I want to point out only that he consciously turned us away from the haunted, quasi-rational world of Pythagoras and set us firmly on the reasonable road of taking the world apart piece by piece to see how it works. Aristotle was a classifier. He developed logical categories into which were divided his observed data. The simplest example of this method is his Scala Naturae, the biological ladder he developed to categorize all living creatures according to their functions. It begins with viviparous man, descending through sub-categories to the oviparous species, and ends with the tiny sea beings produced by what he called spontaneous generation. The quality of Aristotle's biological work is perhaps best demonstrated by an opinion two millenia after he lived. Darwin was greatly impressed.

From Aristotle we inherit immensely rich lists and analyses, and a rigorous methodology. The individual compartments of his logical groups clarify by providing a limited platform for focus, in the same way that a clean glass plate provides a platform for focus under a microscope. Aristotle would doubtless have used a microscope if it had been available. He was probably the first naturalist to dissect animals, a modus operandi not coincidentally associated with microscope use. Separating the specimen into pieces is the most primitive method of 'enlarging' those pieces for the naked eye. Dissection thus has a long tradition in scientific practice, and offers a ready metaphor for the scientific enterprise as a whole which has succeeded in pulling apart physical matter into smaller and smaller pieces until now they are so minute we can only imagine them. We believe, in some ways rightly, that dissection and the microscope gave us the first keys to the kingdom, to the animal kingdom, to the plant kingdom, and through giant sky microscopes to the kingdom of heaven. Not for nothing do we use the term 'microscopic precision' to denote foolproof and truth-revealing exactitude. We have taken the material world, divided it and conquered, and like a crowned victor, our scientific methods are flattered and revered.

Aristotle's gift to us was great. We can trace the advances of modern medicine, for example, back to his early biology. But Aristotle left us with a problem. His categories – divisions and sub-divisions of the natural and cultural worlds and of thought itself – separated reality into pieces for better seeing and understanding. Like specimen plates, these categories enhance our concentration. But the glass plate under a microscope achieves its purpose at the expense of what lies beyond. A clean plate inhibits foreign objects from straying through the examined image. The lens and plate intensify our vision, but rigidly restrict our view. This is the way of rational thought, the way of all science: to dismantle the world into bits and pieces (either literally, or more commonly through mental categories), to scrutinize them, and to draw conclusions. The problem Aristotle willed us is that once we begin to dissect the world, to separate it into fragments and define their boundaries, we also begin to lose a sense of earthly wholeness. Reality consists of discrete parts all right; everyone knows that, because words tells us so. In a way we begin to dissect the world when we learn our first nouns. But a child not yet in the grip of rational thought can call a tree a fish or anoint the grass as ocean, and even adults can build castles in the sky. Metaphor, random memory, association and concrete symbol all release language from the constraints of rational thought and give our reality a marvellous connectedness. Language is really a fifth limb, with sensuality and rhythm, through which we touch the world. Systems of logic we impose from without, though we certainly display an aptitude for them. What logic has given us is the ability to split apart and rearrange the world, to manipulate it to our liking – and often to our distress. Logic allows us to explain convincingly why it is not possible to stop polluting the earth's rivers tomorrow, although we know we are closer to the truth when we use a crude simile and say the water smells like hell. Logic has given us the power to create an enormous abstraction, the blueprint for a huge machine of immense complexity and productivity – the planet we inhabit – and has given us the power to tinker with the plans. Inhabiting an abstraction is not easy. Though some are apparently satisfied with Aristotle's legacy, many of us find life in a blueprint unsettling. Perhaps the philosopher caught an intimation of this modern malaise. It is interesting that he spoke of his conclusions as 'saving' the data, as if he knew intuitively that pulling the world apart left it, and us, exposed to danger.

Pythagoras remains an interesting thinker for our times because, while he shared our modern faith in the mathematical underpinnings of matter, he left the world intact. He was not a classifier and did not dissect reality. The Pythagoreans believed in the unity of all things and in an affinity among all animal creatures. For this reason they abstained from eating meat and followed a diet of vegetables and fruit. If their doctrine of an omnipresent soul passed from body to body seems improbable to me, I nonetheless feel nostalgia and respect for their all-embracing sense of unity. These islands are the right place for such intimations of oneness, I think, since this is where the methods of Aristotle first forfeited unity in favour of partial knowledge. I would not want to reverse that exchange, to yield up my Aristotelian view of the world, because I would not want to live in thrall to Pythagorean-like tenet and taboo, but here on this water-lapped shore the invisible link of Pythagorean oneness communicates a strange appeal. For our divided times, Pythagoras is the philosopher of a healed earth, even though we inevitably approach him partly through Aristotle's divided eyes.

No matter. Aristotle's eyes have discovered many wonders in two and a half millenia. The blood-orange bees weaving around me, long and delicate as dancers, have head, thorax, wing, organs, chromosomes, intricate amino acids, yes, but they are also dancers married to the rocky hills, risen from stray *skoulopetra*, the fascinating fleshy red sea-maggots who dance on the floor of the bay. It is possible to overcome Aristotle's problem without forfeiting his gift. The Greek poets Ritsos and Seferis do it in their best leaping poems. There are others in other tongues. Pythagoras counselled silence, the discipline of the east, but we can also touch the earth's silence with words, plunge back into it with the language of wonder. Imagine a place beyond dissection, a place which embraces all known and supposed time, from the limitless void with its infinity of light years to the first pool of water reflecting primordial constellations, from nascent protozoas to the last ape-man in Africa, and on through the caves and fire-dances and honing of tools to Sumeria, where man first removed words from his mouth and ear and scratched them on a flat plane as I am doing now. Imagine all time, galactic, geological, biological, anthropological, mythical and historical, imagine it all in one omnitemporal place, a sphere beyond dissection, always defying death. There sleeps the silence of Pythagoras. It sleeps within all of us and all that is within us is sown without. The still centre holds. You can find it here on a simple rock by the ancient Greek sea.

8

Travels on Chios

Go to Mesta. Go to Mesta. It has risen to a litany, everyone chanting that we must make the trip, and so we've packed a couple of sacks and headed south. Across the Kampos, past the faded, crumbling mansions barely glimpsed through holes in their high walls or cracks in their unhinged gates, and out into the sleepy, rolling hills of the south, we are going to Mesta.

It is only thirty-five miles on the road from Lagada to Mesta (pronounced Mestá), fewer as the crow flies, but already we seem to have travelled much farther. In fact, we seem to have crossed the water and reached another island. Where the north is severe, hard, mountainous, an oven of hot rock and blasted scrub, this southern landscape is softly hilled and covered with a generous spread of soil. We pass prosperous vegetable gardens, dense stands of evergreen trees, olive groves, and acres of the low, elegantly balanced mastic shrubs. The mastic plant, for which this half of the island was once famous, is still cultivated for its resin, though the spicy glue-like sap no longer fetches much of a price. The mastic villages – Mesta, Pyrghi, Olympi – used to enjoy a global chewing gum monopoly until American synthetics came to the rescue of oral boredom everywhere. A small amount of gum is still made, also an expensive liqueur and a sweet paste which Chian hostesses serve to guests. The paste arrives in a tasty lump attached to a spoon at the bottom of a tall glass of cold water. It usually makes a pleasant mouthful, though not necessarily at nine in the morning.

Mesta is the last village on this southern road before it debouches into the sea. We have traversed the island. The bus driver puts us out in a small dustblown desert, away from all the greenery, then rolls off toward the water. That grey-white wall over there might be the outer limit of Mesta. As we walk nearer to it, we catch our first image of the place, a clutch of older women squatting in the dust. They are all wearing the traditional vizored cowl and blue working apron. One holds her mule limply on a tether. The others have goats. The women smile at us languidly. Everything about them is slow. They give off an air of lethargic contentment, nodding to us from an age before our bus was invented, before we were invented, an age when man moved with his few humble animals and knew no other call.

Stepping through a hole in the grey-white masonry, we step into the village. After five minutes, we lose ourselves. The little streets run every which way, and besides, where are we going? To Mesta. In the north they speak of this village with a touch of awe, a hint of nervousness. They are poor down there, the northerners say, and dirt stinks in the laneways. But . . . it must be seen. Unique in Greece, observes my erudite guide book. In the north, where people are more prosperous from sailors' wages and pensions, they seem to know that Mesta retains a quality they have lost or perhaps never possessed. Go to Mesta, they said.

We walk awhile through the maze. It is right that this place should be a tangle. Perception needs a good shake-up before claiming to see anything here. Built in the Middle Ages, Mesta has not changed appreciably in six hundred years. The inhabitants are doing largely the same work, and in the same buildings, as when the Genoese were their lords. A foreign mind and eye, as much as they can adjust, adjust slowly to the backward lapse in time.

Two thin, shrivelled faces point us toward the central plateia, and eventually we do find it, the anagram unscrambled, the tiny seed discovered inside its gnarled shell. The plateia is the eye of a frozen white storm. Layer upon tangled layer of the Mestan maze surround it. I imagine once this village centre was a bustling place. Now, just before noon, it is strangely mute.

In the single café we are given directions to a house outside the walls which offers rooms for the night. On through the twisted streets we go, another way this time and, with help, we find one of the old gates, pass through it and over to the house with rentable rooms, one of a few new dwellings built beyond the walls. In the courtyard sits someone familiar, Jim McCarthy, the rare American we met last week at Nagos, a sandy beach on the north shore of the island. Jim occupies a room in the house proper. We are given beds in the renovated stable. Well, if not renovated, it has at least been washed out, more or less, and supplied with furniture. We leave our bags with Jim and return to the heart of the maze.

High noon and only three old men sit in the silent square. Mesta is in decline. The men lounge around a table, drinking nothing. Maybe this is not really a café at all. But when I climb up the stairs and look in, I do see a café – empty. Empty tables, empty counter, empty sink, everything is empty. I walk through the emptiness to the back of the long room which may once have held many people, and I find a solitary figure bent over another sink in a small empty side space, a kitchen. She is peeling potatoes. Unreal it is to find a woman with potatoes in all this emptiness. She brings us fried eggs, potatoes and tomatoes, for which we each pay ten drachmas, thirty-five cents, an incredibly small sum, less than half what we would pay up north. Life in Mesta runs very close to the bone.

There is in the plateia now a tall turbaned man, drinking nothing, but sitting at a table. The Turks left Chios in 1912 and although this man is old, it would be his father, not he, who would remember them. In any case, the turban may not be Turkish, at least not directly. The Chiots adopted wrapped head scarves as part of their traditional costume long ago, sometime during the Ottoman occupation. This is the first one I have seen outside the museum in Chios Town. He has a mischievous twinkle, the turbaned one. I think perhaps he is the village jester. They often wear hats.

I swing my chair around and we talk a bit, the usual chat about who we are and where we are going. *Touristes*, they say, but they usually want to know from what country, and whether we are married, and if so for how long and with how many children. The turbaned one is not interested in any of this. He has the demeanour of a sophisticate, and looks bored, like someone from the demi-monde on a private income, though his clothes tell me there is no money. He is suffering from the ennui of poverty, perhaps, but his Greek pride and independence appear to be unbroken. These threadbare old men around the café are endowed with a perverse brand of freedom. Denied any hope of improving their material condition in a poor village, too old to emigrate, they have nothing to do but spend the allowance they receive from their families or the pittance they get from the government, and contemplate the affairs of their plateia and occasionally the world beyond. Life could be worse. A Greek café in the open air must be as good a place as any for an old man with empty pockets to spend his final days. There is companionship here and the continuity of many years.

'What is the crack in that wall?' I ask him. An impressive fault divides the three-storey antique structure facing west on to the plateia.

'*To seismo,*' he replies, '*ogthonda ena.*' The 1881 earth-quake. In contrast to the razed settlements of the north and the collapsed mansions of the Kampos, these southern villages were spared, though the ground here shook fearsomely. He tells me all this as if it were last month's natural disaster, as if he had been watching in the plateia when the wall trembled and split. His grandfather would have been alive then. I imagine an old man telling the turbaned one this tale of the shaken earth some fifty years ago when it would have still been alive in living memory.

Have we seen the church, he wants to know. He will show us. A tour of the church is the last offer I expected from this one. The local bordello, if such a thing existed, would be more his style. A bored jester will do anything for attention. We rise and follow him through the maze. At the edge of the settlement, against the enclosing wall, stands the little church of Palaios Taxiarchis, said to be the oldest public building in Mesta. We enter the courtyard, and the turbaned one reaches for an enormous key, perhaps a foot in length, hidden high on a dusty ledge. '*Ella,*' he says. Come. And he cranks open the ancient door, beckoning us into the dark.

This is another empty room, without furniture, without light. The priest here is a poltergeist. We should have stayed in the courtyard. There was an interesting sense of anticipation out there and the gateway was chiselled through a delicate little arch. I don't like the way the turbaned one is looking at me, though I am not sure why. He waves us forward slyly, or so it seems, and points out the iconostasis, a wooden screen separating the sanctuary from the nave. Up this close I can see the wooden carving alone is worth a visit. Various biblical tableaux are depicted in primitive relief. He is pointing out the symbols of paradise now, Adam and Eve serene, the tree of forbidden fruit, the serpent, then a carved door, and beyond the door a second Adam and Eve horribly deformed, two ghastly beings out in the cold, suffering their fall from grace. I have always liked this story. It may overstate the importance of good food, but it shows with precision how knowledge is acquired at the expense of serenity. The most interesting part of the tale is not the charmed life before the fall, but the moment after expulsion. This is what disturbs and fascinates us. We recognize it. Certainly the immediate aftermath of eviction fascinated the eyes and hands that carved these figures. A witch and an ogre, demented and demoralized, loiter outside the gate, apparently the victims of some sort of devastating primordial lobotomy. The turbaned one is grinning at them. He motions my woman back, indicating that a little distance will improve the scene, and then his long bony arm snakes around and his hand is hugging my woman's bare shoulder. She disengages quickly and puts me between herself and the interloping limb. So this is his hidden retreat, a dark tomb where he comes to look at wooden drama and touch the flesh of foreign women, a touch of paradise, foreshadowing expulsion. He is harmless, the poor lecher, deprived but benign. Inside this unlit church lurk five hundred years of troubled Mestan dreams and tightly knit bloodlines from which a body occasionally escaped into sodomy, bestiality, adultery or the rare touch of foreign flesh. Now there is America, Australia or West Germany where the young can stretch their desire unbound by Orthodox devotion. But the turbaned one is too old to go away.

We leave him at the church gate and wander off through the maze. The narrow Mestan streets are often dimmed by a vaulted ceiling on top of which stand the extended upper stories of houses, but always there are regular oblongs of sunlight illuminating the way. On some streets the ceiling disappears, allowing a full flood of sun. These spaces dazzle the eye, light on white on light on white, the perfect setting for a miracle. It is architecture which makes Mesta unique, architecture and the tissue of light. The blocks of houses here have been termed megastructures, because they fit together as one. An archaeologist uncovering this village in five thousand years might think from the unity of design that it had been an enormous convent or palace, built in a tangle on purpose to confound heretics or spies. Then again, perhaps archaeological interpretation will not be necessary. Perhaps Mesta will survive intact – a happy though unlikely thought. Beauty draws admirers, and admirers speed decay.

We come upon a sturdy roundhouse, a massive cylinder built with thick cubes of dressed stone. Past it walks a Greek leading his mule. He stops for a few words, and when he discovers we are Canadian, congratulates us. It rings a bit hollow, this flattery for an accident of birth. Still, there is something irresistible about a stranger in a strange land hailing you at first sight as a friend. We have been similarly congratulated many times. The Greeks admire Canada because they believe immigrant life there is more humane than in other countries, although not always as prosperous. And they regard Canadian foreign policy as benevolent. The Americans have not been forgiven Kissinger's stand on Cyprus, and the Germans, who flock here in great numbers, have the stain of wartime occupation on them. 'From the Genoese,' he says, slapping the massive tower. The Genoese, it occurs to me, were here long before Columbus was born. Canada dissolves. '*Oraia*,' he adds, jerking his head toward the old stones. We watch him amble slowly down a tilted laneway.

Back toward the plateia now our feet drag, fatigued from the noonday heat. Riding past on a horse the village idiot nods blankly, his mouth slung open in chronic amazement. A female relative follows on a mule. From time to time we pass an aged inhabitant shuffling home, but there are very few people in these streets. The turbaned one said many younger couples have left to look for work. There is no sense of purpose here any longer, no will in the place. The old men sit in the café, the old women on their front steps, waiting for time to unravel a little more. There is always more time. The houses here are old, built to last forever, so that we have the sense of walking through eternity, where the motions of ambition and regret are equally inapplicable. A solitary cat darts across the narrow way with a fat mouse between its teeth and disappears under a rotting door. Above, a baby fig tree tries to grow from shallow rooting in a crumbled domestic wall. Images of a ghost town.

In the plateia we take a cool drink before going back to our stable and trying to sleep. I begin a letter home: 'Mesta is a village whose medieval architecture is protected by law, yet it has none of the gloss and tourist flack usually associated with such visual gems in the rest of Europe. I'm thinking of polished towns like Rothenburg in Germany. The ancient castro tower stands intact, undisturbed by souvenir books, guided tours or tourists in a queue. We were alone there except for an old Greek leading his donkey.

'The village is walled, originally with only one entrance, now several, piracy having fallen out of fashion, the danger gone with the centuries, as have many of the inhabitants. It is quiet here, and a little deathly – the crumbling quietude of desertion and decay. The children flee Mesta for Athens and America. Only the old and the animals shift through the miniature streets, moving every bone slowly, as if to prolong life in a place they know is dying. They are so old, so few and so insubstantial that they are not really here at all, but are imagined, peasants called up from the dead to give us a sense of how life was or might have been under the Genoese, who fortified this place in the 1300s.'

Jim McCarthy has been told all about Mesta by the Fillas family, in whose establishment we are staying. He is relaying to us now what he has gleaned in a week. We haven't met any other travellers as alert as Jim. He is a student of classical history, knows modern Greek and is gifted with an eye and an ear for significant detail. Mesta fascinates him. If not for his law practice in Minneapolis, he says, he would stay here for a long, long time.

We are sitting down at Passa Limani harbour, a couple of miles from the village. This is where the Chian aristocrats scrambled into boats to evade the marauding Turks in 1822. Passa Limani is now a scrappy dead end entirely without character. A few unremarkable tavernas hang their heads by the water. We came here because travellers who think they are enterprising always go to the end of the road. Jim is telling us that the Mestans held a conference last year to determine the future of the village. Loyal natives returned from cities in America, and from the Greek mainland where they had emigrated in search of work. Concern had been growing about a steady decline in the local population. Opportunities for work have been scant for years, and a high proportion of the young has moved away, just as the turbaned one told us. But no matter how far Mestans travel to find a new life, they still feel bound to the village and still feel an obligation to protect it from final collapse. They want Mesta to live, particularly those who now work in Athens, because they want to be able to return here regularly and renew their affiliations to the old life. Jim observes that the village is now mostly an elaborate old folks home, with only two hundred year-round inhabitants, a small fraction of its former size. Until last year's conference, Mesta's future appeared to be no more than a series of sad funerals.

Of those who have emigrated, many are now prosperous. It was decided at the conference that village loyalists, if a government loan could be secured for the balance, would buy shares, as their means permitted, in a passenger ship. The ship would begin a new run from Rafina, near Athens, to Passa Limani, where we are now sitting. The government loan was granted and the ship bought. Two days ago, says Jim, he watched it make a first landing here amid much excitement and revelry. The exiled Mestians now have a lifeline back to their ancestral home, and believe they also have a profitable new business venture. The run from Rafina to Passa Limani takes about half the time of the route from Piraeus to Chios Town. In a few years this may be the more popular route on to and off the island.

Certainly the new ship will bring a flood of tourists. Until now Mesta has been protected from tourism by its relatively remote location almost half a day's journey from the main port of a relatively untravelled island. Now it will be an easy sail directly from the mainland, and many island hoppers will pass through here on their way to Chios Town where they can connect with a number of inter-island boats. This is exactly what the worried Mestans want. Tourism, they hope, along with other local commerce generated by the new boat, will save the village. Probably their scheme is the only way. Mesta, however, will not survive unchanged. We are seeing it in the twilight of its medieval incarnation, before rebirth as a tourist site. Helpless eavesdroppers on the past we are, spellbound by what our senses tell us, unable to turn the flow of things. Go with the flow is all we can do. We are, in a way, last witnesses of this place.

Up the long road to Mesta we walk as night falls, and

then into the maze. Only a few street lamps speckle the black web of these streets. One proceeds from faint light pool to faint light pool, darkness engulfing most of the town. In the spooky plateia a crowd of men sit by the café entrance, many more faces than were here this afternoon. There are also two other tables of travellers.

Over a simple meal the conversation takes a North American turn. Jim attended a baptismal celebration in the plateia earlier this week and was impressed by the open eroticism of Greek dancing, as we have been. Dancing takes us into adultery, the church, illicit physical relationships; and Jim and I argue about physical deprivation, the suffering of chaste young women and those whose husbands leave the island to work abroad or on the ships. (Young men in Greece take their sexual pleasure where they can, without any stigma. There is at least one brothel in Chios Town.) No, I am saying, it is not like religious celibacy at all. Fantasy is not constrained, and for the married women there is sexual memory and sexual anticipation. Besides, our attitude of centring all sex in the genitals, the modern scientific attitude, is hopelessly inadequate as a description of the Greek erotic make-up. All the touching here, among family, among friends, among men in the café, among children (not unusual to see two girls or two boys strolling arm in arm), all this is erotic, though rarely genital. Jim just shakes his head and speculates that there is probably more secret rolling in the hay than we foreigners can imagine from our outside view of things. Probably he is right. What really distinguishes us from the natives at this moment, though, is not our blind eye to their secret matches, but our discussion of the sex drive over dinner. They would, I'm sure, find our serious opinions on the subject baffling, perhaps even offensive. We pay and stroll out through the twisting laneways. I had forgotten how good a conversation with edges can be.

At the Mestan gate we sense we are walking into another zone, another dimension. The narrow channels of stone dissolve into open darkness and there is a change of weather. Inside, the climate is sunsoaked, sheltered, warm. Once through the walls our skin prickles against a cold rush of midnight air, as if we have just stepped out of a handsomely built mansion, or through a hidden tunnel of time. The feeling fits. Mesta is both of these.

In the morning we bid good-bye to Jim and take a last walk through the maze. Along a sun-showered wall, his mouth still hanging open, the young imbecile rides past us again. We poke into some of the ground-storey doorways, every one a stable. Animals live at street level here, human beings upstairs. It is late, almost noon. We are hoping to thumb a ride up to Pirghi, so we make our way out through the walls on to the main road and stand awhile. Although there are no cars within the walls, some traffic passes en route to and from the harbour. At this hour we find nothing. Earlier a few people would have been going for supplies up to Chios Town. The next bus won't stop here for another two hours.

A short bearded man approaches, catches my eye. I see he definitely has us in mind, perhaps to help him with directions. At first glance he looks Athenian. I know he is not an islander, because islanders rarely wear beards, out of respect for the Pappas, who always do. But when I open in Greek, the bearded mouth hesitates uncomfortably and replies in a mixture of English and French. Where are we going? *Vers le nord?* Would we like a lift in his van? He has seen us sitting here, and guessed we needed a ride. So we are off to Pirghi with Michel, his German girlfriend Claudia reading the map.

Pirghi is a disappointment. The largest of these southern settlements, it has lost its character to an invasion of three-wheeled trucks and motorcycles. The traditional geometric designs still decorate many buildings, but village costume, observed by travellers as recently as fifteen years ago, has disappeared. We rouse the custodian of *Haghioi Apostoloi*, Holy Apostles, a four-hundred-year-old Byzantine chapel off the main square, and dutifully examine it. Magnificent Orthodox architecture the little church is, its perfectly preserved domes decorated with saw-tooth bands, concentric arches, and slender columns of marble, all in delicate miniature. Holy Apostles has the abandoned air of a museum piece now, making it both more and less interesting. We move back to the plateia and order lemonade. The heat today is overwhelming. If Pirghi showed more promise, we would look for beds here. To avoid the heat we might do so anyway. This thought is quickly dispatched by a man who enters the plateia looking like a beekeeper. Thick netting draped over his head and shoulders, he carries on his back a tank equipped with hose and nozzle. At the threshold of the square he begins to spray, clouding the air with insecticide, or is it homicide? The death merchant quickly clears the plateia of all bugs and people. A blind customer of this café would conclude that germ warfare was sweeping the island. The four of us scramble out of range, holding our throats, all thinking the same thought – find the van. We do find it, and drive off in a hurry. I wonder how much longer the tank porter will live.

The Frenchman wants a swim. He does not mind driving in the heat as long as we can have a swim somewhere. So we are driving to Lithi, a beach on the west coast. The landscape we pass through is soft and rolling, like the hills on the way to Mesta, dry but green, and much less cutting than the north. Lithi, said our friends in Lagada, is a beautiful place, and so it seems to us when we arrive. The beach is set at the foot of a long, narrow inlet, and the sandy floor of the sea is touchable for a hundred yards from shore. The water, having fried in this shallow basin all summer, is almost too warm. I float here and imagine Lithi's first stone-age swimmers. This warm panful of sea, lodged between two muscular headlands, this generous sandy bottom, must have encouraged a strong belief in mythical beginnings, magical ways. Now there are too many people, and the beach is stained with litter. On the south arm rises the skeleton of what I take to be the first hotel. Better to close one eye and imagine Cro-Magnon Man, or better still Cro-Magnon Woman, knee deep in warm water, head tilted toward the sun.

The Frenchman is restless. Fay suggests we try Elata, a few miles to the south. We'll have to drive back into the interior as no road runs up this coast. She met an American boy in a shop one day in Chios Town whose family had returned to Elata after ten years for a summer visit. The beach was good, he reported, but there was nothing to do in the village, no television, no pool hall, no hamburger joint, nothing. He was anxious to go back home to Pittsburgh, no doubt horrified that only his father's earlier escape had saved him from growing up isolated and poverty-stricken in Elata. To us, however, the place sounds remote enough to be attractive.

The Frenchman loops south. It's not far. We pass Elata proper and head for the beach. He is on a three-week holiday and puts swimming above anthropology. Later we may stop at the village. Corkscrewing down a narrow rocky road, down, down from the hills toward the sea, one hell of a route to the beach. We are spinning a tail of dust out behind and hammering every bolt in the van. What we need is an animal, but then the Frenchman and his German woman would not see much in three weeks on a mule. I ask him how he thinks the vehicle is doing. He shrugs and says maybe we will be walking back.

Elata is on the fringe of the mastic area, and we are passing occasional clumps of the bush. Michel stops to have a look. Resin oozes from slits in the bark and will be collected this month. We peel a sticky crystal tear from the trunk and taste it. The aroma is reminiscent of mothballs, though somehow more pleasing. In the old days the translucent gum we are eating was so highly valued that its cultivators were awarded special status by the Turks. My ancestor described their situation: 'The most celebrated production of Scio is the mastic gum, an article held in so much esteem by the Turks that the Greeks who cultivate the shrub from which it is obtained enjoy several peculiar privileges. They are not subject to pay either tithe or tribute, and are permitted to wear white turbans. They are also tolerated in the use of bells on their churches; and the only public burden to which they are subjected is that of attending to the watch towers on the coast, near to their villages. In return for these immunities they bring annually to the governor a quantity of the choicest mastic, of the value of about fifteen hundred pounds; and the day on which they do this is one of the grandest festivals known on the island. They come in white dresses preceded by musicians and dancers, resembling in the style and practice of their march the ancient processions in honour of Ceres and Bacchus. The mastick gardens are the most remarkable things in the island. Under the shrubs, the ground which receives the gum as it drops from incisions in the bark is made smooth and neat as a pavement.' The earth pans under the shrubs still resemble pavement but, alas, the presentation festival is no more. That old life is long gone. I am tempted to feel nostalgia for it, tempted to believe in lost epochs here, because so little has replaced them. There are few cars in the south of Chios, few new buildings, few new roads. On the surface life looks to be much as it was in 1810. The earth pans remain smooth.

By the time we reach the sand, the weather has changed. A mean wind is howling. The water is choppy, the beach deserted. Michel and Claudia spread their towels, determined to sunbathe, but an hour in the blowing sun suffices. On another day, without the wind, this little cove would be idyllic. Today there are demons down here, and I'm itching to clear out. The Frenchman decides he wants to find somewhere else to spend the night, somewhere with a taverna. Good. He opts for the other side of the island on the hunch that the wind will be dead over there. We're about to pull away when suddenly a man appears and hails us unsteadily. Could we lift him up the hill? He climbs in and launches into a long story about how he almost drowned. From the shape he is in I would guess this accident happened recently, say within the last six hours, but he says it was last year. Perhaps the trauma never healed. He is drunk and quite upset about it all, which has the advantage of taking our minds off this nasty road. Michel decides he has no time to see the village, so we drop our accident victim on the outskirts and watch him wave wildly and lurch into town as the van pulls away. I will always be curious about Elata.

The Frenchman is in a hurry now. He and Claudia want another swim before dinner. I remember hearing about a beach and taverna at Aghia Ermioni south of Chios Town. Maybe Michel is tired, or maybe he has taken a little too much sun. For whatever reason, we are no longer proceeding at a safe speed, but careening through the corners as if ours were the only vehicle in motion up here, and there are a lot of corners. Suddenly we can see the water again. The view from the hill town of Aghios Yiorgos is spectacular. The Kampos, the water and the coach stretch out below, and across the blue channel looms mountainous Anatolia. We sink down through pine trees and olive trees into the ruffled green Kampos, and find our way to Aghia Ermioni. Our hunch was good. The wind is only a light puff here, the water is smooth, the taverna is open.

At dinner we have time to talk. Michel is fluent in German and works as a translator in West Berlin. Claudia is still a student there. They are an earnest pair with simple needs. If they lived in New Hampshire they would probably own a copy of the Whole Earth Catalogue, and perhaps a tract of land, but being European they have no right to such optimism. A siege mentality is inevitable in West Berlin, they say. We conclude this thought where it ends for most earnest people, with an exchange on the possibility of nuclear war.

Having found the few rooms hereabouts full of summering Greeks, Fay and I decide to thumb back to Lagada. Two lifts take us to the far edge of Chios Town, and there we are left alone in the dark. No one is driving up to the northern villages at this time of night. We stretch out on a stone wall with our extra clothes on and doze, jumping to hail any engine that comes within earshot. Finally, just after two o'clock, a taxi stops. He sizes me up, then offers to take us home for the cost of his gas. I'm baffled by this windfall until a few minutes later when he says, 'You are the foreigners? I know. You live in the house of Irini Vavouli.' The man is Irini's cousin, from another village, but he has heard of us, and is therefore happy to give us a lift. That we are taking him miles past his own destination is unimportant. The Greek words for foreigner and guest are the same, and often, as with the cousin's gesture tonight, their meanings overlap.

★   ★   ★

In the morning we meet Michel and Claudia at the centre of Chios Town and follow the road into the mountains toward Nea Moni, a monastery recomended for its mosaics. Almost all the literary travellers to Chios have visited this place and recorded their favourable impressions. My ancestor was one of the few not to go. I surmise from the anti-clerical comments in his book that fifteen kilometres uphill on muleback to see a church seemed to him greater devotion than any organized religion deserved. For us the trip is no effort at all. The little road up into the high interior behind Chios Town has recently been paved.

My erudite guide book says that 'Nea Moni is the most important monument on the island, and is considered to be of international rank; its paintings and architecture place it amongst the most significant Byzantine churches in Greece.' It's difficult to know exactly what the word important means in this context. Sometimes important means illustrious, often it means influential, occasionally it means wealthy, and once in a while it means essential to the sustenance of human lives. It can also mean pompous. In the eighteenth century, I gather from my literary sources, Nea Moni was at least influential and wealthy, but how much of its past glory remains we are not sure. I am encouraged by Professor Bouras' high estimate, however. His little guide book, which I recommend to travellers here, has thus far proved refreshingly candid.

Up and up we climb. This is some of the highest terrain on the island. The view of the flats below, when we can catch a glimpse of them through the pine forest, is breathtaking. Outside the holy precinct, parallel to a long picnic bench, the Frenchman stops his van. The bench may indicate the popularity of this place with tourists, or it may have been installed for worshippers on devotional outgoings – no sign of either group today. Our van is the only vehicle in sight. Although the road is paved no buses run here, except on Sunday mornings for the weekly service.

We tread lightly through the cobbled courtyard. Incessant ringing of cicadas. The tapping of our feet on stone the only human sound. This monastery has seen better days. Walls are crumbling and some roofs have collapsed. Built in the eleventh century, endowed by the Emperor with ample estates and special revenues, Nea Moni grew to be one of the most famous churches in the Aegean. Like so much of old Chios, it was reduced to a memory by the 1822 massacre. Although largely rebuilt following that disaster, it never regained anything like its former prominence. George Finlay, the doyen of historians for the revolutionary period, describes the debacle thus: 'Two thousand persons had sought an asylum in the fine old monastery of Nea Mone, which is about six miles from the city, secluded in the mountains towards the west. The Turks stormed this monastery as they had done that of Aghias Minas. A number of the helpless inmates had shut themselves up in the church. The doors were forced open, and the Turks, after slaughtering even the women on their knees at prayer, set fire to the screen paintings in the church and to the woodwork and roofs of the buildings in the monastery, and left the other Christians who were not already slain to perish in the conflagration.' As well, much of the ancient treasure was looted. The sacred vessels, the archives, the library, all were stolen or destroyed. The monastery remained abandoned for many years, then gradually was repopulated, only to be dealt another staggering blow by the great earthquake in 1881.

We poke through a dark doorway into the building with the octagonal dome, a design said to exist only on Chios and Cyprus. I take this to be the main church. Supporting herself against the back of a decrepit chair, the gnarled old nun beckons us with two enfeebled fingers.

Come here, come here, she seems to be whispering, before I fall over and die. In fact, however, she has plenty of spunk, and proceeds to talk our ears off, describing in detail each withered artifact sealed in glass cases along the corridor. I have made the mistake of admitting to a slight knowledge of Greek. So few visitors to this country study the language that the natives have almost no experience with people who speak their tongue imperfectly. Other parts of the world have had in the recent past either waves of immigration or waves of colonial administrators, both of which have left a heritage of linguistic multiplicity. Here there were only the Turks, a long time ago, and they were never on this island in great numbers. Most islanders assume one either speaks Greek or not, nothing in between, and in keeping with this rule the old nun has placed me among the fluent, a grievous error. I am exasperated by her incomprehensible antiquarian enthusiasm. She has only one tooth, lodged front middle in her upper gum, and her words find it impossible to skirt this little fang. They want to go right through, with the result that they reach me split and mangled and wet. I understand about five per cent of her spiel. There is a long story about the Holy Virgin which I miss entirely. She is oblivious to my protests, this old woman. When I say I have not understood, she tells me to translate to my friends.

'How many live here?' I ask her.

'Five,' she replies. 'Four nuns – and one Pappa for the church.'

'How many were here before, when the monastery was full?'

'Eight hundred,' she whispers sadly, lowering her eyes. O Byzantium, how the mighty are fallen. She does not say so, but nuns are a relatively new acquisition at Nea Moni. Until the last war only monks and priests lived here. We have by now seen two of the other three black sisters, both shrivelled and frail. The establishment, I calculate, has at most another ten years of inhabited life, unless the fourth nun is younger than these three, or unless replacements are found.

She leads us into the church proper to see the famous mosaics. Scaffolding has been erected in front of several walls for repairs. A few mosaic figures which survive intact are magnificent, but the damage is generally more severe than we had been led to expect. The remnants speak of fine work, past glory, but mostly of time forgotten, of an age ending, of decrepitude and death. Back out in the corridor I point to the saint depicted on a postcard and ask if we may see it. No. The pressed silver portrait is not on public view. It is locked in one of the back rooms.

'Why?' I want to know.

'Because there are thieves,' she shrieks, implying with a scornful look that I might be one of them. 'Come.' She takes us out into the blinding sun and points to a doorway in another building. 'There,' she says. 'Go to the rectory.'

We go to the cavernous rectory and find a long stone table and stone benches built into the slab-stone floor. The marble surface of the table is worn at each place. We choose seats. I don't know what the others are thinking, because the scene has struck us all dumb, but I am imagining myself eating a meal, and am quite enjoying it until the old nun reappears at the door. She sees us scattered on the benches, staring silently at her.

'What are you doing?' The voice is indignant. 'You may not sit here.' Suddenly we are out in the sun again. 'Go to the water house,' she commands, sending us in the direction of another outbuilding. We obey, and peer through the rusted grill at a vast underground chamber with elegantly capitalled columns standing in old brown

water: the ancient cistern. It is all a disappointment, Nea
Moni; or is it? Apart from the few remaining mosaics,
none of the artifacts on view here is very splendid.
Everything has wasted with age. The decay is sad, yes it
is, but something in me finds it a relief. Any monument
like this which has not been diminished after nine or ten
centuries is bound to be intimidating, a mockery of the
human lifespan, an enormous burden of time. Nea Moni
reassures us that stones are fallible and finite, that while
humanity may endure forever, all its history will not. This
must be one reason why ruins appeal to their inheritors.
Ruins let us touch the past without chaining us to it.
There is a sense of bereavement in fallen walls, but also a
sense of freedom. The heart admires durability, but also
clamours for change.

The three monks who founded Nea Moni were inspired
in their choice of a site. Although buried deep in these
pineclad hills, the retreat enjoys an unmasked view
through the cleavage between two peaks. From the courtyard we can look down all the miles to the sea and across
to Turkey. Surrounded by the not-too-demanding past of
tumbledown buildings and heaving pavement stones, we
sit awhile, then leave the nuns their long green silence.

Michel continues along the same road, steep and contorted and no longer paved. There is supposed to be a
ruined medieval settlement at the end of it. Some say this
town is the most interesting on the island. On we roll,
dipping and turning and climbing and arriving nowhere.
Then around a bend we see it, the grey outgrowth on top
of a rocky peak, as unlikely a site for a village as man's
mind could invent. The sun is searing as we walk up. Our
books say that Anavatos was abandoned years ago. I can
believe it. That leaves the question of why anyone ever
came here in the first place. The terrain all around is
ungiving rock, and we are miles in from the coast. No

doubt they came for the same reason that islanders throughout the Aegean came inland during the Middle Ages: to escape the pirates who ruthlessly plundered all villages by the sea. This mean refuge is a measure of the appalling fear those pirates must have instilled.

A woman materializes in our path. She must be mad. Either that or we are hallucinating. No one could possibly elect to live here, not when there are dozens of more habitable places within a day's walk. Chios is not the Gobi Desert. There are plenty of fertile strips scattered elsewhere across the island. Here only a miniscule needle of green withers in the gully below, and a swatch of old olive trees droops on the far slope. There is no credible source of food, at least not that I can see.

'What do you want to drink?' demands the woman. This strikes me as ludicrous. Is she inviting us to a party, or conducting a survey of local drinking habits?

'*Tipota*,' I say. Nothing. Best not to get involved with this crazy apparition. She might have relatives.

'Tell me what you want,' she insists. 'I have the café here. Coffee, lemonade, wine, anything.'

'Where?' I ask, incredulous.

'Right there,' she gestures. At the bottom of the pathway sits a tiny white house which I had taken to be a shepherd's cottage. 'Come,' she continues. 'Walk through the village and then take a drink.' Automatically I say yes. If she really does try to run a café here, the least we can do is buy something from her.

Up the path we climb, between two rows of collapsed dwellings. All the roofs have caved in, although most of the walls still stand. The living areas are small, space for two stools, a sleeping platform, a pail, the mule's wooden saddle. Life here must have been very tight. The path winds up between more fallen houses and passes a church with its roof still in place. Debris litters the dirt floor, but an altar remains, and some smudged icons. Up a few more paces and we reach the summit, high over all these ghosts.

On the way down Fay and I leave the other two and investigate another face of the hill – more rubbled roofs, empty rooms, heavy stone blocks neatly fitted in rows, so much grey matter both vertical and collapsed, so much grey abandonment that we're startled when we see the pink face watching us gently from a terrace above our path. The face nods.

'You are strangers,' it murmurs, meaning, I suppose, that we are aliens, beings from another world. The face belongs to an old woman who shuffles over to examine us more closely.

'You live here?' I ask. Yes. 'How many others?'

'About fifteen in this village now,' she says, almost inaudibly. 'But in the old days, eons ago, there were many more people here.' She actually does say eons, or rather *aiones*, which is the Greek for century. She knows these things, she reports, because her father told her and his father told him and so on back over the generations. My only knowledge of Anavatos is that the insurgent Samiots retreated here in 1822 on their way to the west coast where they fled the angry Turks by sea. This woman gives us a more detailed account of that event. The Samiots passed through quickly. No one gave them a second thought. A couple of days later came Easter weekend, and the villagers launched their annual celebration, the most important on the Greek calendar. There was the usual excessive feasting and drinking. When a thousand-strong force of Turks arrived in tardy pursuit of the Samian trouble-makers, they took Anavatos by surprise. The local men had only sticks and stones for weapons. Some women tried to hide in trees, but were mercilessly hauled down and put to the sword. Everyone but a handful of escapees were slaughtered. These few survivors later returned and reestablished life here.

Intense horror has taken hold of this woman's features, as if she had witnessed the massacre herself. These islanders display a remarkable capacity for personal attachment to history. She continues, telling us about the June 4th earthquake which destroyed the village permanently in 1881.

'Now we are only a few people,' she says, 'because the houses have fallen and there is little food.'

We exit uneasily. It seems heartless to leave an old woman here, but someone must be looking after her. The house was in good repair, she had fruit trees growing on her terrace, and she claimed not to be alone, though where the other dozen or so inhabitants lodge remains a mystery. We see two more liveable houses, and the so-called café, nothing else. Maybe the houses hold large families.

The café door is open. We crawl in, mice through a mouse-hole. Everything is miniature under this roof. Even the people are small: the little woman who met us earlier, her small husband, and a squat old cousin who is deaf and dumb. He carves wooden staves, apparently for a living. There is a bundle of them by his side, and one unfinished in his hand. I recognize these rods. The Pappa in Lagada has a staff exactly like them. Opposite the rod maker Claudia and Michel have squeezed into undersize chairs. Two small men sit at the only other table. We order and drink up, and the little woman brings our bill, well padded. We are paying for the losses here, the abandoned houses, the dead customers, and the ones who long ago fled.

On the dirt road between Nea Moni and Anavatos splits a fork to another village, and the consensus now is that we should take it. With any luck there will be a more prosperous café with some food. The Frenchman rolls us into the plateia of this place, called Avghonyma on our map, and we step out into deathly silence, not a human being in sight. Avghonyma is clearly not deserted, although at the moment it appears to be. The stone block houses, something like those in Anavatos, are all well maintained, as is the church. A solitary adolescent creeps into the plateia, stares at us, then makes for the shaded wall opposite. There he taps obsessive feet to private songs, music with apparently demented rhythms. The sun is drumming hard and soundless on the square. Mid-afternoon and everyone is asleep. We scout around for a café, but find nothing, which is impossible. The café is the heart and sex organ of every Greek village. Life collapses without one. Unable to find it, we munch a dry loaf on the church steps. Avghonyma seems choking and hopeless. The stillness here is not the romantic aban-donment which gnaws at Anavatos, but the mute remote-ness of provincial narcolepsy. The silence here breeds demented inner music.

I leave the others and walk into the back streets, but not alone. The seedy adolescent is following, for what reason I can't tell. We round a corner and he overtakes me, sly and challenging, stops and cocks his head and jigs his hand in the way Greeks do when they want to know your purpose.

'*Volta*,' I say. A walk. The explanation doesn't satisfy him. He continues to dog me through the laneways, though I see nothing I might steal, no chickens, no goats, no grain, nothing but closed doors and silence. He comes beside me again, very agitated.

'*Fithia*,' he says, with a crazy leer. Snakes. '*Great big ones*.'

'Where?' I'm not a snake lover, as he seems to have guessed.

'Everywhere,' he exclaims. 'Through the streets, on top

of the houses, in the trees. We have many snakes here, big ones, very bad.' He gestures toward the roofs and a couple of old pine trees in an attempt to conjure vipers. I scan it all with great care. No snakes. Obviously he wants me out of town. Perhaps he's just poisoned everyone in the village. His eyes suggest a capacity for such things. Or perhaps there's a strong local strain of xenophobia. In any case, he has succeeded in unnerving me and I'm leaving. As the municipal greeter, he certainly makes a refreshing change. Avghonyma is well protected from the perils of tourism with this one on the loose.

We're travelling north now, toward Lagada, which the Frenchman and his woman want to see and where they can stay the night. We'll take the slow inland route, stopping in Pitios, a small dot on the map, and Homer's legendary birthplace. Down the hills into Chios Town we descend, and then climb up again on another switchback road, up and over Mount Airos and on to a flat rocky plain. This is the way to Volissos, the largest village in the northwest, so the road is good until we come to the fork leading to Pitios. Then it's all dust and bumps.

Though poor and remote, Pitios turns out to be a contented little place boasting four cafés. This may be a very, very old site – Pitioussa is one of the ancient pre-classical names for Chios – but its buildings are only as old as the Genoese. The remains of a Mahona fort stand on a rise just beyond the houses. The legendary affiliation with Homer is, of course, just that – a legend. No material evidence exists for or against. We walk up the central laneway, lined with old men and women sitting on their steps, and I ask one of them how old the village is. He says maybe eight hundred years, then shrugs. No one really knows.

On the other side of Pitios the road shrinks to a donkey track. Don't worry, says the Frenchman, the van likes adventure. We lurch down it and suddenly swing on to a view of the sea, our sea, the water we swim in and gaze at every day. Lagada lies a couple of miles directly below Pitios, although the track will make a long triangular detour before it arrives. We have just come over the hard hills which push against our little valley, forcing it down close to the water. I had thought, rather whimsically, that these hills were impenetrable. Now we have ridden through them and ridden through most of the rest of the island, all of which has been penetrated for thousands of years.

9

September Wine

'But you think Lagada is the most beautiful village, yes?'
asked Grandmother Roda anxiously after hearing of our
travels across the island. Yes, we replied, it's best here,
and we did not have to stretch the opinion. Lagada has
been good to us. There is no other valley by the sea to
match it, not on Chios, and the people here have almost
broken our hearts with generous hospitality. We might
easily have searched for months without finding such a
place. There's no accounting for luck.

The sun is a little weaker now and we are having
occasional cloudy days. Around us the hills boom daily
with gunshots, hunters killing birds. Except for my wife
and me, no one swims any longer. They say the September water is too cold. Grapes are appearing in large
quantities on muleback and truck. The summer population has left for Athens and America, reducing the village
by half. In a few days we too will be leaving.

The cove is deserted now. I go at noon and swim alone,
and then we swim together later, just before the hill
shadows grow long and cool. The other day I looked up
from the water at the blazing sky and saw a half moon
hung in the blue, as if I'd tripped into a timeless sea where
day and night intermingled, waking jumbled with dream.
The army was no longer stationed around the next bend.
That beautiful little plain called Delphini where soldiers
used to camp had been returned to the birds and wild asses
who held sway there in the beginning. The black pigs I
saw on the beach at Paros appeared there too, descended,

I think, from the pigs Homer's men had to inhabit at Circe's mischievous bidding. An apparition those Parian swine were. A little Irish girl stood beside me on the balcony and said: 'Look at those people by the rocks,' as children often do, without apparent reason. I looked, and saw some ordinary people standing beside rocks across a little bay, then turned back to talk to her mother. A few moments later the child exclaimed, 'Look, they've changed into pigs,' and we looked and saw that the people were gone. In their places pawed half a dozen small black swine. They were snorfling the sand, looking, I suppose, for their lost human shadows. It was also a question of shadows for me out in the cove. Floating through the turquoise liquid I watched my own silhouette move along the sand under layers of aqua light and feared my final disappearance into the enchanted sea.

We are doing last things now. To Sikiada we returned for a bottle of Psara wine, the best we have tasted here, a litre for less than a dollar. We'll take it for Athens. Walking down the hill from Sikiada toward the coastal road late in the afternoon, we saw the failing light pitched halo-like on to Turkey's mountains and skinny Oinussai's tail. At that hour of low-angled sun the little island looked uncannily phosphorescent. I can't explain the marvelous glow except to guess that a dormant god with windy lungs had just opened his eyes on this forgotten corner of the globe and decided to blow away the dust of centuries and have a better look. We'd never seen the opposite side of the channel spilling forth such light, although there were a few other evenings when the weather had been clear and the mountains visible at sunset. I was impressed by their loftiness each time I saw them and remember once remarking to the Pappa as we walked down our street together how fine a profile the Anatolian peaks made.

'No Yiorgo,' he said reproachfully, 'for us they are not beautiful. That land used to be Greece. Now it is Turkey. We are enemies.'

'But the mountains were Greek many centuries ago, were they not?' I replied, thinking his comment showed a highly exaggerated sense of history. Asia Minor has not been politically Greek since the fall of Byzantium. Irredentism based on the boundaries of the Byzantine Empire is hardly what the world needs now.

'No,' he concluded, looking pained. 'It was all Greek until 1922. My grandfather came to Chios from there.' He had been referring, I understood then, to the established Greeks who inhabited Anatolia from ancient times through the Byzantine and Ottoman Empires until the official exchange of populations between Greece and Turkey in 1922. A million refugees flooded across the Greek border in the years immediately following the treaty. For the Pappa and others like him, Anatolia would always represent something taken, something lost.

In a curious way, those mountains evoke the harsh contrasts of 20th century Greek society. They remind us of the soldiers camped on this and other islands, prepared to repel the Turks who reportedly maintain a huge force ready on the other side. The army is a symbol of Greek alertness and resolve, but has also been the instrument of conservatism and official repression. Paradoxically, the Anatolian mountains also bring to mind Greek communism, the political current most alienated from the military. It was the refugees from Turkey in the twenties who were among the most malcontent of the Greeks and who helped to organize in that decade the Greek Communist Party. The ideological split which opened wide between Right and Left in those years clawed the country through half a century of repressive dictatorships, civil war and unstable democracy until 1974 when a constitution was devised that appears to have satisfied a broad consensus of opinion. Ideology divides parties still, but the gap is narrower now and less volatile. The Communist party, suppressed after the civil war, has been officially restored, but claims only a few elected members of Parliament.

Some villages are more politically candid than others. Vasiley, a captain who lives down our street, drives his car daily to Sikiada. Only there, he says, can a man engage in frank political discussion. The people of Lagada are less forthcoming with their opinions, either out of fear or from lack of interest. We have seen signs of fear in conversations, and certainly it would be the logical consequence of political experience in these parts. I have the impression that many here would rather forget about politics altogether than risk more deprivation and bloodshed. Many of them spent World War II in refugee camps in Egypt only to return to another armed struggle, this time Greek against Greek, which lasted five more years. With that history and the ever-present Turkish threat, some political reticence is understandable. Only once I heard partisan politics discussed in a Lagadan café, and never until I talked with Vasiley would anyone speak more than half a minute about the civil war. Some of the young men, eighteen and nineteen, discussed politics with us, but always in whispers, and always with the caution that we must never quote them. Their sympathies were socialist, and they were afraid of reprisals – obstruction of their careers or rejection of their applications to enter university. Once, when a village youth and I were discussing the present government, how much it differed from the Colonels' regime and how much had remained the same, he suddenly jabbed me in the ribs and clammed up. Two army privates had turned the corner and were walking toward us, harmless young men like himself doing their military service as he would soon have to do, but harmless or not, he was taking no chances. What the army didn't overhear couldn't be used against him.

The most striking example of hushed political opinion came to light for us only this last week. We were in the harbour celebrating the village saint's day. It was a party like all the others we attended through the summer, tables bubbling with jocularity, amplified music taking the town by storm, and all night the energetic dancing. None of it was as interesting as the old man beside us. A neighbour of ours, he had seemed inordinately quiet and retiring for a Greek. We passed him many times sitting alone on his little verandah staring into space. The night of the party, after half a litre of wine, he told us his story. Like thousands of other Greek communists, he had gone into exile in Poland for thirty years following the civil war. Only recently had he been allowed to return. His wife had brought up their children by herself. He had never known them except as infants. Calm and philosophical, he seemed not at all disillusioned with his political choice. Life in Poland had been very good, he claimed, and if he had stayed, the Polish government would have given him a pension. Here in Greece he had nothing. He meant he was without money, but it appeared that he was also without friends. Sustained now by his sons and once again living with his wife, he had reclaimed what is more important to a Greek than ideology, economic security or even friendship – his family. They treated him, in public at least, with the same respect accorded all heads of family in the village. But they never mentioned his past, and never made reference to his politics.

Our last lunch with the Pappa this week focused on a fantastic fish. We had been there the day before when a messenger arrived to tell the Pappathia she had won the village lottery. He handed her the prize, a fish stolen from an exaggerated fish story. It was red, enormous, and endowed with the ugliest submarine face possible. Hieronymous Bosch could have painted such a fish. It must have had a surly, carnivorous voice under the sea. Overcome, the Pappathia took the dead creature in her arms and laughed and danced through the house, chuckling that she had recently dreamt about just such a fish, and that we must have brought her luck by being in the house when the messenger arrived. We must come, she said, and help them feast on it.

'Eat, eat,' chanted the Pappa. The fish was submerged in the deep again, deep saffron yellow soup, its red snout nosing over the edge of the pot. We ate last year's olives from the Pappa's tree and this year's tomatoes from his garden. The herbs for the soup had been picked in the hills around our valley, and the fish had been landed by one of the local men.

'You have everything here,' I said, 'your food, your work, the sun and the sea, all without leaving this village.'

'Yes,' the Pappa nodded, clearly pleased with the idea.

'You have fruit trees, olive trees, animals, birds,' I went on. 'You even have serpents.' The hills of Chios are said to harbour giant snakes, though I never saw any. 'Perhaps this island was the site of the first garden.'

The Pappa looked puzzled. 'The first garden comes after winter,' he declared uncertainly, 'after the rains.' He must have thought my Greek was failing me.

'I mean the very first garden,' I continued. 'The one in the Bible.' He was still confused. 'Paradise,' I said, lapsing for a moment into English.'

'*Paradisio!*' he exclaimed, and a troubled look moved into his eyes. 'No Yiorgo, paradise was not here. The first garden, the first men, they were not here. They came from a southern place, a place called Israel.' His answer was deadpan, literal, fundamentalist and unyielding. I had been making idle conversation, not very witty, but not at all mocking. The Pappa, unnerved by my hint of sacrilege, anxiously steered us back on to the approved course. Leaky's African near-men have not yet ruffled the thinking of these islanders. Here we are still the Children of God, descended from an ancient desert tribe.

Only once did I meet a local man who went beyond the confines of the Orthodox intellect. He was a doctor from Chios Town who had the government contract for medical care in several villages. Having heard that a foreign writer was in Lagada, the doctor asked to see me one evening when he was making his rounds. We sat on a neighbour's terrace, sipping coffee and discussing literature. He had studied medicine in Paris just after the war, and his time on the Left Bank had apparently marked him for life. He kept throwing Sartre's name into the conversation and was eager to know what I thought about existentialism. Sartre's answer to the same question ran four hundred pages, and since my own views on the subject invariably bore me and my listeners afer a minute or two, I told the doctor that only Sartre deserved to give the subject more thought. I felt sorry for this self-exiled intellectual, an outsider in his own land. He had been working on a play, he said, for ten years. It was difficult, but he was almost finished. Had I heard of Tennessee Williams? He was the greatest existential playwright in the world. For a few months, until meeting the doctor, I had forgotten the terrible single-mindedness that scholarly pursuits so often bring. His stubborn grip on existentialism depressed me. The narrowness of Orthodoxy could be no worse than this, one strict ideology replaced by another. I couldn't see the necessity of either system that evening. The cicadas were chiding the fallen sun. A flock of sheep grazed slowly across the far hillside in ethereal purple light and the water in the bay was still as a staring eye. At that moment no arrangement of ideas by gods or men could have made any difference at all.

The grapes had been drying on little Markella's grandfather's roof for two weeks. She knocked on our door just after sunrise the day of the pressing and led us down to the house. There we danced in the grapes with Markella's mother, her aunts, an uncle, her cousins, and other assorted children. The grandfather whose house it was had sunk the metal frame of a winepress into concrete on his roof for this one day in a year when the family's wine was made. Beside the press he had built a lip enclosing a concrete basin. Inside the basin we danced, wearing boots reserved for grape-dancing, and when we had smashed a pile of grapes sufficiently, the grandfather scooped them into his press, and the pool flowed into a funnel and then down a hose to pails on the terrace below. Markella's frail old grandmother tended the pails.

Another grandfather had come down from the hills to watch. Many of the grapes had been harvested from his terraces on slopes behind the village. Once we visited him there in his simple hut by the vines. Inside there was a bed, a table, a chair; outside, a bench and a crude fireplace for cooking. He was the only one we met from the village who treasured his solitude. We climbed up the hill with his daughter-in-law Katina and her mule one day, bringing him supplies. Who were we? he wanted to know. Katina tried to explain, but he seemed unable to understand why we had travelled so far to spend a few months in his valley, and why we had climbed the hill to see where he lived. I found his accent impossibly thick, and he understood none of what I tried to tell him, or so I thought.

The morning of the wine-making he sat gravely to one side of the roof offering advice on how best to tighten the screw and stomp the grapes. He was older than the other grandfather and not as strong. His own dancing days were over, but the light in his eyes signalled a rare pleasure at the scene of this annual ritual. I sat with him awhile watching Markella's mother sweep the pressing floor with an aromatic whisk made that morning with sprigs and thyme. He looked at me intensely for a moment, the way we might look at a strange object just fallen from the sky, and then he gestured over the hills.

'Do they have wine?' he asked.

'Wine?' I echoed, turning my eyes over the hills where he had been pointing. Somewhere near the horizon he lost me.

'Wine,' he repeated. 'Do they make wine in Canada?'

I tried to imagine how he pictured my country. Quite likely he had never seen it on a map. Every other place, rumoured and real, had to be compared to this tangible valley by the sea.

'The winters are very long,' I said. 'It is difficult for the grapes. We buy wine from other countries. From Italy. From Greece. . . .' He nodded sadly. I had confirmed his suspicions about the world beyond these hills, beyond the sea, a wineless, tasteless world of grim winters and gloomy men. That was not at all how I remembered it, not the warm golden days in September when a few people at home do pick wild grapes and make their own wine, and when the leaves paint hallucinogenic colours on the hills. I saw myself flopped in the grass one autumn afternoon, a jug of cider lying empty somewhere nearby and the blue and white canopy above whirling extravagantly past my spinning head.

'But we grow wonderful apples,' I said. 'And we make wonderful apple wine.'

'Apple wine . . .' he murmured, seemingly reassured by the thought. 'Did you say *apple* wine?' he asked a moment later. There was a mischievous smile on his face, as if such a fine idea had never occurred to him before. He put his hand to his ear and cocked it questioningly, the way the Greeks do when they want to signify alcohol or madness.

'Yes,' I replied, 'sometimes it is very strong.'

'Apple wine,' he murmured again, this time with a crinkly grin. I might have said gold from donkey droppings, so taken was he by the idea of our cider. I could see the apple trees growing in his eyes, pushing up out of the snow, enormous red apples against a crystal white landscape, and I could see the two of us dancing on someone's roof in Canada, dancing in the apples, and drinking large cupfuls of last year's apple wine.

At six o'clock, just before sunrise, the bay was sombre. Two fishing boats lay still on the water like deadwood floating in a swamp. The leafy floor of the valley was a deep ruffled green, undulating folds of olive tissue for a tired giant to stretch on. Above Turkey's mountains the sky was flushed with the pink scarf of dawn, while overhead a half-moon still gleamed.

We rose early because this is our last day here. I am sitting upstairs with my notebook, on Irini's verandah. Yaya Roda is in the chair beside me, telling of her life during the war, her escape across the water to Anatolia and thence to a refugee camp in Egypt. Before the Germans invaded, Lagada was much smaller than now, with a sister settlement just out of sight in the hills behind. Yaya Roda lived in the twin village in a house she described as beautiful. After the war, when everyone returned from Egypt, they found the inland houses destroyed by the Germans.

Fay is walking back to the house now with an armful of presents from neighbouring women whom she has visited for the last time. The bus will be coming soon. Yaya

Roda hobbles down the stairs and walks with us along our street to the island road where we'll board the bus. Irini is there with the children, and so are some of the neighbours. The Pappa shakes my hand ceremoniously. '*Sto kalo*,' he says. Go to the good. The bus hurtles down the hill, and we throw in our bags. The women are weeping now, infectious tears, and I am on the verge of weeping myself as the bus pulls away from this valley that we will probably not see again. We have left many places together in the last ten years, she and I, but we have never left such a big-hearted place as this.

We pass through the village proper and mount the southern slopes, up, up. One last look and the valley is gone. The road winds down the coast along vertiginous cliffs. This is our last ride, somehow portentous. A narrow switchback climb up one particular rocky face always made me uneasy. The more so after we heard that a taxi flipped over the bank in July, and I've been wondering whether we'd make this last run safely. Of course we do, just as the villagers almost certainly will for the rest of their lives.

In Chios Town there's half a day to fill. We wander through the old Genoese castro where Turks and Jews lived during the Ottoman period. A tiny Turkish cemetery survives here with tombs of prominent Moslem soldiers and administrators who died away from home. Outside this medieval quarter we climb a nine-storey apartment building raised sometime in the last decade. From its roof we can see the landowner's vast garden, the harbour, and the handsome library, all the town in fact, and beyond to the table mountain. The red tiled roofs and one remaining minaret lend this bird's eye view a strong Turkish flavour, although only Greekness is bustling in the streets below.

No more to be seen here, no more to be said. At dawn we sail for Lesbos.

10

A Painter, a Castle, Some Haunted Trees

The isle of Lesbos rises in the mind, gossamer, voluptuous, taboo. Lithe women lounge together in the sand caressed by glistening eunuchs. Parrots mate with pigeons in the golden lemon groves, and fecund red orchids stand twenty feet tall. Under olive trees the dark side of desire spins elegant ballads pledging the flesh to its own elusive ends. We all harbour dim memories of love entered, love denied. The losses of lust, and its clinging hopes, these inhabit the uneasy island of the heart we touch when we think of Lesbos.

The real earthen Lesbos doesn't live up to these dreams, not at all. Sailing up from the south, I could see the terrain here was a little greener than Chios, and not quite as rugged, but I can't say there was anything voluptuous about it. Mytilene, the main town, is pleasant enough, not at all sleepy, but no hotbed of libido either. I like the horseshoe harbour and the amphitheatrical hills behind. The waterfront is an attractive place to sit. Although we arrived only a day ago, we sense already that the people here are looser than in Chios Town, less withholding, less suspicious. Chios belongs more to the East.

After casing the harbour we checked into an unusual waterfront room. Most Aegean hotels have been built since the mid-sixties when tourism began to boom, but this one is antique and falling down, so old I'm tempted to call it a hostelry. We had read about it in a quaint old travel account published in 1912. The Grande Bretagne it was called, now translated into Greek as the Megali

Vrettania, offering the cheapest rooms, the most memorable architecture (giant statues on the façade), and the rankest air in town.

'Is this the old Grande Bretagne, the one that's been here since 1912?' I asked the owner, who was also the desk clerk, wedged into a tiny reception room on the second floor. A Lesbiot, he spoke English with an Australian accent.

The owner examined me carefully, perhaps wondering if I had been trying to insult him. Anything old, unless it dates from classical times, is regarded as inferior by most Greek islanders. To have real cachet, a thing must be *moderna*, brand new.

'This is not,' he said slowly and without intending irony, 'the Grande Bretagne in Athens.' It was good to have our whereabouts confirmed. One gets muddled in foreign countries. It's always possible to board the wrong boat or disembark prematurely at the wrong port. Just the same, I hadn't for a moment thought this was the Grande Bretagne in Syntagma Square, an imposing structure at the centre of the capital and probably the most expensive hotel in Greece. At a loss as to how I might continue the conversation, I went back downstairs to the street. People who convey simple information in negatives are blind to the difficulties they create for the rest of us. There is a flavour of guilt and anxiety to the negative, reminiscent of the defendant's plea in a courtroom. The worried man at the desk did look guilty about something. What I can't say. Maybe he felt ashamed to own such an old piece of property, or maybe he had an unmentionable past.

We met another strange one in Mytilene. She glided out of a Somerset Maugham story set in the East Indies seventy-five years ago. I exaggerate the time and place a little because she was an exaggerated character. Suddenly she appeared, standing over our waterfront table, watching us sip cold drinks.

'I can see you're new here,' she twittered. 'I'd like to give you this little map of the city.' We thanked her warily. Since we'd begun our travelling again, it seemed everyone was making a fast grab for our pockets. Stupidly, I thought this woman might be doing the same.

'I came here thirty years ago to teach,' she said. 'Right after the war.'

'Oh,' I said remotely. We had a bus to catch.

'I never left,' she persisted. 'I think I made a mistake.' The accent was genteel British. Everything about her was faded, her eyes, her skin, her clothes. She wore a faded hat which she, and Maugham, would have called a bonnet. Did she wear white gloves? I forget. She left the impression of a gentlewoman of indeterminate age who wore white gloves and face powder.

'That's too bad,' I replied without much feeling, aware of my callousness but not prepared to relinquish our plans for her gloomy tale of self-exile.

'Yes,' she murmured, stepping back and wilting a little. 'But I don't mean to intrude. Really I don't. I'm sure you've things to do. One doesn't find many people who speak English, you see. I should have gone home before. I know I should have. Now all my people are gone. Everyone is dead.'

I tried to muster some sympathy, but had already decided we would have to escape her. She was too polite and talked too much, always a bad combination, and worse among British gentry. She came across as one of those spinsters who believe they're well bred and assume good breeding is a license to bore anyone within earshot.

'You'll like the island,' she continued, though we still had not invited her to sit. She paused for effect, then blurted: 'The people aren't very nice.' It was this dottiness about her that intrigued me a little, and interests me even more in retrospect.

'Well, I'm here alone, you see,' she explained, 'which isn't very good for invitations. I've made a mistake, that's all. Silly of me, don't you think? I should have left years ago. I know I should. But here I am. One has to make do, I suppose.' Her presentation had all the marks of a ritual – the token gift of a map, the strange costume, the lines polished from repetition. No doubt a similar routine was played for other new faces on other days. As soon as she left I felt enormous pity for her and upbraided myself for my meanness. Besides, we might have learned something about the island from her, and I remain curious about the life she leads here. There is no visible evidence of an expatriate community in the town and only a sprinkling of tourists in the streets. I wonder whom she has found to sustain her.

We left punctually for the suburbs, not sure what we would find. The government brochure says simply, 'It is of interest to visit the village of Varia where the popular painter Theophilos was born and where there is an art gallery containing eighty-six of his paintings.' The notion of an art gallery on this or any other Greek island seemed quite fantastic. Mr Argenti's display of family portraits had been one eccentric aristocrat's labour of self-love; almost any other main town in the Aegean would be hard pressed to pay for the upkeep of such a place, let alone build and fill it. In a way this is no shortcoming since Greece has produced only one modern painter of note. The others, the might-have-beens, have all been squashed by poverty. Theophilos ought to have been squashed too, since he was as poor and ill-schooled as most of his countrymen, but Theophilos was one of a kind, a peripatetic misfit and free spirit whose impassioned inner eye disregarded both his own and his country's chicken-scratching deprivation. He was dismissed as a lunatic and loafer by the villagers of Lesbos, and was apparently taunted and reviled. How could a grown man play with pots of colour when there were still good fish to be caught? Once, it is said, his tormentors shook him down from the ladder on which he had balanced to work on a mural. None of this abuse stopped him from painting, which he did until his death in 1934.

The bus dropped us at the side of a lonely road. There was no art gallery in sight, only a narrow laneway which we assumed would lead where we wanted to go. At home the town would erect another pernicious sign, defacing the solitude and stealing any sense of discovery. Greek silence is better. We walked up the laneway, wondering what we'd find over the rise, and then came to a plain whitewashed outbuilding, perhaps an old stable, or the local farmer's tool shed. A woman was fanning herself on the wooden bench.

'Where is the museum?' I asked.

'This is the museum,' she answered without any feeling. Take it or leave it.

Inside we found several small whitewashed rooms, though not much of the white was visible. Every available square foot of vertical space had been hung with Theophilos' paintings, all crammed together, like fugitives hiding in a basement. The first impression was of visual crowding and visual suffocation – thin, hungry canvasses locked shoulder to shoulder in a dim, airless room. What light there was trickled in through small square window holes. The paintings were stretched on plain artist's slats without protective covering and without explanatory notes. But the images were surviving, and their creator probably would have been pleased to see them protected from the sun and rain in this humble gallery. He had humble needs himself. A primitive, itinerant decorator, he painted on whatever surfaces came his way – wood; old tins; rags; the walls of houses, shops and tavernas; and toward the end of his life when a few people had begun to recognize his gift, he painted on these canvasses, depictions of peasant life and re-enactments of events in modern Greek history. Some of them are very bad pictures, and none have mastered the laws of perspective, but many are brilliant in spite of their technical limitations. In the best scenes, the people are mobile and breathing. I can still smell the painted bread that a painted baker was taking from his oven.

The poet George Seferis, an early admirer, explained this artist's gift: 'Theophilos gave us a new eye. He cleansed our seeing. . . . He has something about him that is like the trembling of the dew. Maybe he is not a virtuoso; maybe in this sphere his ignorance of technique is great. But he has this enormously rare thing, this thing that before him was impossible to achieve with a Greek landscape: a moment of colour and of air, held there in all its inner life and the radiation of its movement.' (*On the Greek Style* – George Seferis.)

I am looking at postcards of his work now to jog my memory. We bought them from the massive woman at the door. It is appropriate that his scenes should be immortalized on these paper rectangles. From time to time he worked from postcards himself. I'm playing his game, taking the images full circle, though I cannot renew them as he did. They are stamped with his vision. Postcards, lithographs, natural scenes, anything that caught his eye he used. Here on the table I have an island minstrel with his dog, set against lyrical swirls of scrub and rock; fishermen knee-deep in a bay lifting their net from grey-blue water into a boat whose prow drifts out just beyond the picture's black-lined border; and seven peasants shaking purple olives from the trees and gathering them from the soft, buff-coloured ground. These are images which capture the strong, slow heartbeat of Greek seeing and breathing, and they do belong in a simple whitewashed room, without frames, without labels, without pretentions or distractions from beyond their time and place.

We had heard confused reports about another museum, apparently just opened. Farther down the little road, we found it, a new two-storey building that would be the pride of any French or German town. Out there in the ragged Greek landscape the place appeared to be a surrealistic mirage, which may have been intended. Its inspirer, Efstratios Eleftheriades, or Tériade as he is known to the art world, co-founded in 1932 the influential surrealist review *Minotaure*, and was otherwise a mover and shaker of the pre-war French art scene. Before and after the war he edited *Verve*, a lavish and influential periodical devoted to the established names of contemporary French art, and it is the pages of *Verve* which are displayed in this Open Book Museum. *Verve* was a showcase of virtuosity. Picasso's light-fingered drawings line these walls, along with Matisse's magically simple sketches and Chagall's colourful daydreams. Gloomy Rouault and Miró the mime artist are here, and so are Bonnard, Léger and Giacometti. Tériade was born on Lesbos and chose to preserve a complete run of the magazine's illustrations on his native island. It was he who encouraged Theophilos toward the end of the painter's life and who assembled his primitive canvasses in the whitewashed stable down the road. Not many people see either of these collections, but those who do must remember two of the most unusual galleries anywhere, one perhaps unique in its simplicity and the simple intensity of its works, and the other a visual cantata erupting in the wilderness, completely out of place and therefore all the more lucid. Walking the *Verve* museum, I thought of our common fantasy, about being marooned on a desert island, and that one book we must choose. Whatever the choice, its pages would take on unforeseen dimensions, just as these French images, so familiar now to museum-goers all over Europe and North America, take on a strange new vibrance in the solitude of this Greek pasture. Far away from critical fakery and double-talk, away from the flash and hucksterism of dealer and vernissage, the painted images along these walls speak their own minds, unprogrammed serendipitous thoughts, and encourage the onlooker to do the same. Tériade's paper *Verve* dazzled us, and there were no flesh-and-blood distractions inside the rooms. Two village women, probably employed as custodians, lingered together out on the front steps. Otherwise, we were alone.

On the north coast at Mithymna, some thirty miles from Mitylene, we've taken a room. Distances are relatively long here. Lesbos is the third largest Greek island, after Crete and Euboea. Ten million olive trees, twelve million, twenty-four million, the written estimates vary, but a bus ride through the interior leaves no doubt – Lesbos grows a lot of them. Olives and their oil are the chief exports here. I'm glad I like the tart little pods. There were days in Lagada when the vegetable truck never came and we lived on cheese, local tomatoes and Lesbian olives. I thought they would taste even better here on home soil, but no, they're worse, shrivelled and bitter. Perhaps the best ones are sent away. I begin to see the argument of one travel writer who quit the island after only a few days with the comment that there was no enjoyment in con-templating a sea of olives. But there are consolations in the landscape: the two inland gulfs, for instance. We passed them on our way here, Yera and Kalloni. The bus breaks out of the dry, tree-shrouded olive plain and brushes past the head of Yera, a giant impassive pool enclosed by pale marshy meadows. Near the shore grow poplars and other benevolent greens, all whispering a quiet vegetable calm. Like an undiscovered valley Yera is, the kind of place where evolutionary miracles ought to happen, where jumping fish should be so enamoured with the look of the land they would immediately grow four paws and climb out of the sea forever.

Mithymna is a pretty spot too, or rather must have been a decade ago, and for all the decades before that. Built around the crest of a hill below the still impressive remains of a Genoese castro, the town is a jumble of cobblestone streets and squat medieval houses, many with spectacular precipitous views. In the mid-sixties tourism was consciously developed here, and now there are souvenir shops and handicraft and jewellery boutiques selling any sort of gimcrackery a bored northern holidaymaker might want. Just as the town has become a commodity for vacationers looking for cheap sun and quaint Greek atmosphere, so the tourists have become commodities for the villagers. On our way down from visiting the ruined castro, we were beckoned by an old Pappa who invited us on to his terrace for coffee. We chatted politely for a while, though he was not much interested in our attempts to speak Greek. He did not really seem interested in us at all, I thought. In fact, he seemed distant and confused, perhaps a little senile. When the Pappathia brought out her box of embroidered doilies and he coherently pressed us to buy some, I realized it had been only the embarrassed dementia of salesmanship clouding his mind.

My favourite place in Mithymna is the overgrown public garden, always deserted, beside which stands an unkempt pink-plastered mansion, its skin all crumbling now and its huge iron doors cracked. Inside the mansion in one small room is the public library, where we found Henry Miller's *Colossus of Maroussi*, still one of the best travel books on Greece. I've been re-reading it here, enjoying again his insane enthusiasm for Greek light and landscape, his infantile rages and extravagant lusts. Another travel book on the shelves, *Lesbos the Pagan Island*, solemnly documents the story of Mithymna's metamorphosis in the sixties from a quiet fishing village to a busy tourist resort. I wanted to leave as soon as I read about the mysterious removal of the harmless local lunatic who, it was feared, might disturb the tourists. Nothing disturbing can be found here now, and nothing compelling either.

In the morning we walk down the road out of town and stick out our thumbs. Not much traffic is going west, because not many people live out on that coast, but eventually a trucker stops and we climb up beside him. Yiorgo is his name, going to Eressos, near Sigri where we are headed. An Athenian, Yiorgo has a six-month government contract to work on harbour improvements here. Does he like Lesbos? He shrugs, replying that it's always better to be home with his wife. He's fifty-five, an age which must give him a memory for the war, so I ask him if he fought and what he thinks of all the Germans now travelling in his country. For the last three years, Mithymna, like many popular island resorts, had as many Germans in its streets as native islanders, and I'm curious to know how the Greeks now feel about their war-time masters.

'Yes, I fought,' says Yiorgo, 'but the war is finished and the Germans have good money now.'

'Then you've forgotten the war?'

'No,' he says firmly. 'I have forgotten nothing. I remember very well the friends they killed. But what can we do?' *Ti na kanomai.* What can we do. It's an expression heard daily in these islands, and denotes not laziness or impotence, but a protective resignation, accumulated over years of foreign rule and domestic poverty. The Greeks are a proud people, but they have little time for impossible wishes or futile resentments. We've heard the same answer from others. The war is over and Greece needs foreign currency. It is a pragmatic view, but also demonstrates a sense of tolerance.

Yiorgo drops us at a barren crossroads and disappears in the direction of Eressos. Sigri lies a few more miles from here, along the other fork. Going on eleven it is, no trees in sight, no shelter, no shade, only this doomed expanse of dust and donkey shit. Our bags double their weight in the midday heat, so we elect to wait for another ride and park on rocks by the side of the road. Nothing happens. Two, three hours, we sit and pace. A solitary mule scampers past, and the hot wind blows dirt from one hill to another, but no human beings arrive. This might be a good sign, indicating the romantic remoteness of Sigri, if only we had some way of getting there. Our landlord in Mithymna said scathingly that Sigri was a bad place, with no meat or vegetables, only fish, and sometimes no bread. I put this down to local pride and the usual antipathy any Greek village feels for all others within a day's journey, but now I'm not so sure. This empty intersection is giving me second thoughts. Maybe Sigri is so remote they'll have no food for two more mouths. Certainly no one is trucking anything in or out today. Maybe extra people are unwelcome and we'll be eating more of this blown dust for dinner. Many dark maybes run through our heads at this dark junction, but after a while none of it matters. All either of us want after a while is a glass of cold water. When the man in a little blue pick-up truck rolls over the hill in our direction, we don't much care where he is going, as long as he takes us with him. He does. In the open wagon of his fish truck we speed through the remaining hills to Sigri and the sea. Lesbos is largely green, not as green as Samos, but more fertile than most Greek islands. As we near Sigri, the land changes dramatically and we are back into the hard, dry rockscape, typical of Aegean terrain.

Arriving on the fish truck turns out to be an advantageous entrance into this unprepossessing little place. We climb out and wander over to the only taverna still open, whose owner has been watching us through a window.

'You wanna sty fra few dies?' he asks in thickly accented Australo-Greek English. 'I'll git you a room chipe. Best proice.' He gives us some water and bread and cheese, and then disappears to see about the accommodations. Sigri is not so isolated after all. A few tourists come in July and August, and a modest hotel with ten rooms has been built for them. Like many of the new hotels, this one looks jerrybuilt and ugly, but it's somewhere to sleep. The taverna keeper returns and says they'll fix us a good price. We're the only foreigners in town now, and besides, we came in on the back of the fish truck.

After sleeping we walk to the ruined castro, passing on the way two public water troughs decorated with Moslem script, remnants from the Ottoman days. The village is small, with perhaps fifty houses, not all of them occupied. It lies away from Turkey on the west coast, so we can see the sun setting from on top of the castro's torn battlements. I like this old fort. My mate sits meditating on the dying sun, a pastime which often depresses me, so I descend the ramp and poke into the tiny rooms which huddle black and airless under the ramparts. Troglodytes and rats must live here, though they're all lying low tonight. This is the best preserved castro we've seen on four islands. It was built by the Genoese and used later by the Sultan's occupying forces. A lintel with Turkish script has been inserted over the gateway.

Lesbos rose to prominence in the sixth century B.C. under the benevolent despot Pittacos, later regarded as one of the Seven Sages of Greece. The poet Sappho was his contemporary. (In the minds of some she haunts this island, but I can't find any sign of her. It is estimated that only one per cent of Sapphic verse survives, all in fragments. The substance of the poet, her writing, has all but disappeared, and so has her presence here.) After the golden age of Sappho's time, Lesbos formed a succession of makeshift alliances with various Aegean powers. The island was several times taken by the Persians, then by the Ptolemic Empire, and then by the Romans. Lesbian history is much the same as the history of other Greek islands – a long tale of one forced allegiance after another. The Byzantine Empire, which held the island in the Middle Ages, ceded it to the Genoese Gateluzzo family in 1355. It was the Gateluzzos who built the forts at Mytilene, Mithymna and here at Sigri. In 1462 Lesbos fell to the Turks, who controlled it for four and a half centuries.

The Gateluzzos built well. Those thick ramparts look as though they might easily last another six hundred years. I wonder if the local plenipotentiary wanted someone to see his stone bulwarks and remember the grandeur of Genoa. Probably not, but lying on a massive stone ledge, my mind does turn to them, all their gore and greed reduced to serene desuetude now on this abandoned cape away from all the world's games. A feeling arrives often in Greece that the wiliest machinations of men and their most intricate designs for power are never more than little vanities beside the relentless onslaught of planetary time. The empty castro at Sigri brings on this feeling and seems to echo the poet Blake's clairvoyant verse –

> To see a world in a grain of sand
> And a heaven in a wild flower
> Hold infinity in the palm of your hand
> And eternity in an hour.

We wander back through the darkening laneways and sit outside to eat. Another couple of lately arrived travellers have taken a table nearby. We invite them over for wine. Not having arrived on the back of the fish truck, they are paying more than we are for their hotel room, which leaves them a little discontented, but then they didn't have to wait hours in the midday heat for a ride. From Germany they are, medical students at Gottingen, and they have driven to Lesbos in a rattletrap Volkswagen. Wolfgang has picked up a few words of Greek, including some verbs in the present tense, a rare accomplishment for three-week tourists here. Sabina is his silent partner. We like them, even though they are quite a solemn pair. When I mention that we're planning to find a boat to take us across to the island in search of petrified trees, they suggest we team up.

In the morning I talk to the friendly taverna keeper who in turn talks to a boatman. At ten o'clock we push off from the quaint little harbour, all its rocks arranged as perfectly as if a sculptor had designed them. Because Sigri sits away from the Turkish coast, relatively safe from land-to-land bombardment, a new deep water harbour is being dug with heavy machinery. Meanwhile this natural mooring cove is still in use. We putter across the calm channel to an islet opposite the village and then our boatman leads us down a path on to the rocky carapace that covers the islet's middle. Remains of a petrified forest lie here somewhere, a rare phenomenon on earth. We've read three accounts of these stones, placing them variously at one, four and ten million years old. It's all the same to me. Our guide says he knows where the best examples are lodged, so we follow him down a cleft and look to where he proudly points. Someone's enormous misplaced erection, an uprooted tree trunk, cantilevers out of bedrock, frozen in time. It is pink and orange and crystal brown, grainy and somehow fleshy. Come, says the boatman, there is a better place. We follow him over the crest and down into a small sheltered cove littered with tree stumps. The stumps are solid rock, coated with stony bark and stamped with year rings. The sea laps them as if they were ordinary rotting deadwood, but time has laced their lithic skins with a wild kaleidoscope of colour. Uncanny, this little cove is, haunted by the ice age. One feels a mammoth may lumber out of the sea at any moment. Perhaps these logs induced supernatural visions in the days before paleontology and radio carbon dating. Perhaps if we stood here long enough, we too would turn to stone and last forever.

On the way back across the channel, our boatman says the people of Sigri have always known about the trees, but not until 1956 when some articles about them appeared did travellers begin to come in search of specimens. Now the islet is a sanctuary.

We run into the Germans again after dinner in a smoky café. Like them, we've been drawn in by the music. The driver of the fish truck is here, playing his bouzouki, but after a few more songs he puts the instrument down for the night. He is too drunk to play. Another old salt, flushed from years of sea and ouzo, staggers past us and out the door, puke dripping from his nose. All the men here are bleary-eyed and dour. Not to disappoint us however, the fish man, who is also the proprietor of this café, feeds some money into his jukebox, and the music begins again. A moment later the village idiot lurches in, grinning madly, eyes askew and tongue distended, like a dog home from the chase. Several drunken men clap their hands as he enters. They challenge him to dance, which I take to be heartless taunting until I see he is delighted with their attention. A drunken voice bellows what step to perform, and then the idiot picks up his inner beat and executes a magnificent imitation of a Greek jig, arms weaving, fingers snapping and feet kicking high in the air. The reason he is moving to an inner beat and not to the jukebox is that he is deaf. For us this results in something like aphasia, the melody saying one thing and the idiot's body another. When the music ends, he continues to sway to his own inner song until someone steps up and collars him, shouting that the dance is over. Contented, he sits down with the other men. The mute simpleton who bides his time in every human heart has just taken a bow and left us humble. Not much happens in Sigri after dark, but they make the best of what they have.

With the Germans in the morning we drive to a secluded sand beach. Yesterday, nosing along cart tracks in their old VW, they came upon it, empty, quiet, clear-watered. I remember something Jim McCarthy said down on Chios. 'We are the last generation to see the world in anything like its natural state.' No sign of humanity lingers here, not so much as a footprint in the sand. Behind the beach is a swamp and then a small plain sown in what looks like clover, emerald green. Such lush fertility is unusual in these islands. So are the fauna here. Sandpiper-like birds dart along the shore. In a pool by our rocks and in water by the swamp large turtles take the sun on sandbars. A couple of enormous lizards freeze, then scamper up the rockface as we drop our things. In the salt water we see tiny stripers, larger grey fingerlings, and the dorsal fin of a creature some two feet long. I like to think this is where Aristotle studied fish, though in fact he is said to have taken advantage of the calm inland gulfs across the island. Probably there was more wildlife when he was examining nature than there is now. Our most poignant animal stories were created in those times and on these islands. Aesop, some claim, was a Samian. Others say he didn't exist at all and was invented by historians. In any case, the fables did spring out of pre-classical Greek culture. I doubt there were lions, foxes, camels, apes, bears and wolves all on one island, but there must have been a good stock of visible wildlife on the loose. The stories convey a keen sense of the animal world.

Wolfgang informs us today that he is a conscientious objector and has so far managed to avoid military service. The Frenchman we met on Chios avoided the army too. He told them he was crazy, and produced a fake psychiatrist's report to prove it. I am wondering about the significance of our meeting two pacifists within two weeks. We haven't come across any gung-ho scorch earth people recently. I seem to run into them all the time at home, but here everyone feels it possible for us to get through the days without murdering one another. This says a lot for Greek light, Greek landscape, Greek generosity. Wolfgang picks up his guitar and sings quietly for a while, the perfect pacifist. When I think about it, this place is almost too idyllic. Something in me half expects an air raid. It doesn't matter whose planes. Plenty of accomplished bombers are waiting out there ready to take up the slack. Still, our beach must be a low priority on anyone's list. Aesop's turtles reassure me when I go to sit with them near the reeds. They counsel a narrow view: enjoy the sun-baked solitude here. It's a rare find.

We spend the day lolling and swimming, and bounce back to the village as the sunken sun is painting a broad yellow stripe across the sea. It was a fine day and we ought to sleep soundly, but we won't. The distraught guest next door to us curses imaginary adversaries all night and bangs on the walls. He is one of the workers on the new wharf, separated from his wife for too long. The only bus out of Sigri leaves at seven a.m., so we pass up the bouzouki and turn in early. A little after two our sleep is ended by a violent smashing sound, then another, then again. He is breaking glasses or bottles and grumbling loudly. The door to his room slams. Soon he is back and the smashing begins again. Fay says she is tired of these crummy hotels. She wants to get out of the country.

We doze on the early bus and doze away the day in Mytilene. Evening takes us through the spirited old town, dense with activity. 'The chaffering Levant,' says one guide book, and so it is. We pass a barber shop built into one corner of the ruined mosque, a forge and several carpentry shops, hand-made brooms and baskets, a coppersmith with pots and pans and handsome grinders, a bell maker at work in a small black hole, bakeries with huge piles of hard bread, fish stalls and vegetable vendors, everywhere people scurrying and jostling, a salty market life even at dusk. This is how we are leaving Lesbos, and it's a good way to go, a taste of Turkish bazaar before we sail away west.

11

From Athens to Rhodes

Constitution Square, or Syntagma as it is locally known, has long been the principal tourist hangout in Athens. Most of the year, Syntagma is an annoying place. I have been there in spring, summer and fall, and I've always been a mark for café waiters, street corner hawkers, homicidal cab drivers and wily pimps. Beyond the square, however, this is a likeable city. The Athenians complain about the endless traffic jam which clogs their main streets from dawn to dusk, and they complain about the poisonous air. Both complaints are justified, but still I enjoy it here. Athens is alive and sensuous, and at the same time relaxed and undemanding. The hypertension of New York, the moneyed masquerade of Paris and London, the stiff formality of Madrid, outside all this languishes Athens in a world gracefully unordered, approachable and warm.

An old hunchback sells roasted nuts on the corner. Down the street a blind man clutches a pole, lottery tickets attached from top to bottom. Another man with good eyes is selling the same worthless paper a hundred yards away. Shabby stalls offer poorly worked leather and straw goods, and cheap plastic trinkets are available on nearly every street. Men idle in the cafés. Away from the downtown in residential neighbourhoods, women can often be seen carrying metal pans full of food back and forth from the local bakery where they pay an oven fee to have their meals cooked.

Life here is looser than in other European capitals

because the Greeks are generally easy and informal, but perhaps also because Athens is still relatively young. The oldest national centre in Europe was reborn very late. When John Galt visited in 1810, there was no city here at all. 'It looks,' he wrote, 'as if two or three ill-built villages had been rudely swept together at the foot of the north side of the Acropolis, and enclosed by a garden wall. The buildings occupy about four-fifths of the enclosure; the remainder is ploughed, and sown with barley.' After the War of Independence, in 1834, Athens was named the capital. It was then a town of only three hundred houses, and remained a small settlement until the 1920s when hundreds of thousands of Anatolian Greeks, expelled from Turkey in the official population exchange, raised shanty towns on the outskirts. Since the end of the civil war in 1949, villagers from across Greece have been pouring into the capital in search of a better life. This rapid expansion over the past thirty years has pumped the number of inhabitants up to three million and has left the municipality unable to provide some essential services. Serious flooding in the rainy winter damages buildings and even takes lives from time to time. In summer the downtown air is unbreathable, because public transportation is poor and the streets are jammed with cars. Despite these problems, and the obvious overpopulation which causes them, I have encountered less caged snarling here than in other, better equipped cities, and more friendliness. I think we could spend years in Athens, but Fay thinks not. In any case, she is leaving to go to language school somewhere else. I'll be travelling alone for a while.

Early one morning we take a cab out to the airport. Soldiers with machine guns are stationed at strategic points throughout the complex, reminding us that we are close to the Middle East. The thought doesn't make me feel any better about her flight to Rome. When I go, I'll go by boat. A customs officer examines the papers, then waves her through. In half an hour she'll be airborn. This is too abrupt a parting – nothing else is done so quickly in Greece. On my way out to the highway, the sky is spitting water. It's a sad morning.

Back in the city the rain has lifted. Later I'll read at the Gennadion, a rich antiquarian book collection, but the building will still be closed at this hour. My bus drives past the National Garden, not far from Syntagma Square, and Henry Miller comes to mind. Forty years ago he wandered through these grounds, enthralled. I don't know why we never looked at them.

No one is walking the garden paths early this clouded morning. All the world has gone to Rome. The trees are tall, forty years taller than when Miller was here, and the paths are slim and shadowy. Nothing is precisely pruned, nothing planted in rows. Like Greece, the garden is untamed without being savage, ungroomed without being sloppy. A seed is a wild thing, this place asserts. Let it grow unchecked. I hear faint rustling and smell the more pungent aromas of another kingdom, so I follow my nose through the zig-zagging trails and find some clustered birdhouses: one cage full of canaries, another with parrots, a third with quail. Farther on strut a pair of peacocks. This is birdland, and I am a freak who has lost his feathers. The beady eyes are staring at me, an overgrown featherless goon – without a mate. I flap my arms in mock flight, and they stare back in disbelief.

Past a honking elk and down a path to the duckpond: scores of fowl quack and skim across the smooth surface of an oriental pool. Two human beings are here as well, throwing bits of white bread into the water. People are walking and penetrating the garden. Time to go. The nearest exit gives on to Amalias Boulevard, not far from the Parliament. Here I pass the Evzones, guards in ceremonial dress who march with impressive exactitude for the tourists' cameras. They do make a colourful picture with their enormous tassled shoes, white stockings and fustanellas, but I can't help smirking when I come upon this scene, the Evzones with their finely tuned footwork and well-groomed dress, and tourists freezing the image for their friends in Frankfurt or Milwaukee. This is Greece, they will say, only it is not Greece at all, at least not the Greece I've come to know. The Greek style is entirely opposite to the style of these guards. Like the National Garden, Greece is casual, spontaneous, often unruly, sometimes exaggerated, rarely precise. The Evzones are a harmless piece of folklore.

Every Saturday morning below the Hotel Orion, a small establishment in a residential neighbourhood, Kalidromiou Street sprouts an abundance of fruit and vegetables. The market runs for several blocks and piles the pavement with food. My bag fills with apples and oranges and grapes. With *tieropietes*, the cheese buns sold everywhere in Athens, and the fruit, I can fix a good lunch. One of the many endearing qualities of this city is that it allows a visitor to eat cheaply. In the evenings I dine at a modest taverna down the street for about two dollars, the price of bread and meat and vegetables and a metal cup of wine. Perhaps I sound like a skinflint, but that is an unnecessary psychological explanation. The truth is less complicated. There isn't much money in my pocket.

   The day before sailing back out to the islands, I relax on the Orion roof with a cheese bun and an apple, watching the Parthenon shift colours under a shifting sky. October it is now, and still hot when the sun shines. An archaeologist from Indiana sits across the terrace reading his Greek novel in the original. Every summer for eight years he has been coming here with his wife to dig, and his Greek is fluent now. We discussed bookishness among the Aegean villagers and in the Peloponnese region where he works. Actually we discussed the absence of bookishness. It occurred to me as I watched across the terrace that in four months he was the first person I'd seen reading a book in Greek, aside from scholars in the libraries we visited.

'It's a question of availability,' he said. 'They can't get books, so they don't read them.'

I said I thought it had more to do with tradition. Literacy is a relatively recent achievement for rural Greek communities. The habit of retreating into a world of print has not had time to develop. But the archaeologist was bubbling over with American do-all optimism.

'Nope,' he insisted, shaking his head. 'What they lack is books. These people have tremendous respect for their writers, even though they rarely read them. Everyone has heard of Kazantzakis, and a lot of people know about Seferis, not about his poetry mind you, but about the man and his Nobel prize. I'd like to see a masssive program of book production – select a dozen titles by the best writers and make them available at reasonable prices. Then you'd see people reading.'

I don't share the archaeologist's missionary zeal. My mind's eye sees these books piled for several years in an Athenian warehouse. Rotting and rat-infested, they are eventually used as landfill for a government-subsidized rifle range. Still, I've some respect for his optimism. He is a teacher in the winter and probably a better one than I ever was.

'It must be a difficult country for poets,' I said. 'There's overwhelming social pressure to conform here, and poetry requires such a large capacity for dissent. Poets need to be able to see things in new and disquieting ways.'

'Yes,' he replied. 'The way of the world here is always the old way.' He thought for a moment. 'But they do have poets, you know, and good ones – Seferis, Ritsos, Cavafy, and others. A helluva lot of interesting writers for such a small country. And I think I can tell you why. These people are all in love with their language.'

The Alkion was a stinking old tub, but that didn't matter. I was sailing south to balmy Rhodes. Everyone praises this island, friends of mine who have seen it, and travel writers I've read. The fortified town of the Knights Hospitallers of the Order of St John of Jerusalem is said to be an outstanding example of restored medieval architecture. A great siege of this fortress conducted in 1522 by Sultan Suleiman the Magnificent, and a much earlier siege conducted by Demetrius Poliorcetes against the ancient Rhodians in the 4th century B.C. are two legendary events in Aegean history. Demetrius, impressed by his adversaries' fighting courage, made them a gift of the enormous war engines he had used against them. With money raised by disposing of this equipment, the ancient Rhodians underwrote the construction of a huge statue of the Sun God – their famous Colossus. Said to have stood 105 feet high, it collapsed in an earthquake after only fifty-six years erect and lay for centuries in pieces. Eventually a scrap dealer from Syria employed nine hundred camels to cart the fragments away.

As we sailed up the coast and around a small northern cape, the history of Rhodes felt closer. From a distance I could make out the rectilineal silhouette of the Knights' medieval keep and battlements. We might have been a fast cutter from another century racing to defend the walls. But in reality, as the Alkion rumbled nearer, I realized that what I'd actually sighted was an outline cast by another rectangular age – our own. The once lush city of Rhodes has become a grey garden of stillborn, concrete blocks, hotel after hotel after hotel, the transient castles of our age. For those who like highrise glitter and swarming beaches, this island is now among the most popular of Mediterranean holiday spots.

In one relatively small section of the city huddles the old town of the Knights. Much of it was restored by the Italians, who occupied Rhodes for thirty-five years until 1947. The architecture, splendid though it is, loses out to the commercial clutter of boutiques and souvenir shops lining almost every major street. Half a million tourists stop here annually, roughly ten times the resident population of the entire island. Some of these visitors are very rich. Rhodes is the only Aegean island where painted women with thick fur jackets and heavily jewelled hands are a commonplace. They can be seen occasionally in the streets, but more often in the luxury hotels or at the casino. In the harbour, their men sip cool drinks aboard expensive yachts. The age of the Knights is long gone, but so is the tranquil Rhodes of thirty years ago evoked in Durrell's *Reflections on a Marine Venus*.

I went to Camirus one day and watched lizards scamper through the hot ruins. This was one of the three pre-classical settlements on the island, not a spectacular ruin, because so little remains, but with the advantage of being miles away from the city's concrete towers. I was putting in time. Rhodes had begun to depress me. Contrary to what I was told in Athens, a daily caique does not run down to Karpathos, only the weekly steamer. I had several days to wait.

On the city beach, the first time I walked there, a camel shuffled in the sand, a ridiculous solitary camel. Beside him stood his keeper, a Greek dressed as an Arab. The keeper had with him a stepladder. For two dollars a tourist could mount the misplaced dromedary, and for another five a picture of the mounted fool and beast would be snapped. I can't explain why, but the camel never left my mind as long as I stayed on Rhodes. I'd be walking through the harbour or licking stamps in the post office or buying cigars and suddenly I'd find myself guffawing at the exiled animal and his fake Moslem master. They somehow summed up the sad wanton feel of the whole place.

As almost every visitor to Rhodes does, I went to Lindos. The acropolis there offers a striking prospect over the sea, or so many pictures suggest. The bus poured us out on to a large asphalted parking lot heavy with cars and people. Several soft drink pedlars were doing a brisk trade. Pushing my way up the jammed laneways to the top of the village, I eventually gained the acropolis. Many other bodies were milling about the old stones, so the famous view was difficult to locate, but after a search I dutifully looked over the much photographed precipice. Below lay a manmade wonder, an enormous and growing hill of soft drink cans. Fuck this, I thought, and clambered down in a hurry with the idea of catching the same bus back to town. But the bus had left.

Outside of Lindos I thumbed for a while. Dozens of smug northerners passed in rented vehicles without so much as a nod, and I began to wish them watered gas and broken axles. Not that there was anything to do except wait for the steamer to Karpathos, but I was tired of standing in the sun and watching people with money cruise comfortably past me. It was demoralizing. A stubby grey man finally stopped and invited me into his red mini-jeep. Immediately we discovered common ground. He hated Rhodes. A middle-aged Irishman, he was holidaying while his wife tended business back in Dublin. He found the island uninteresting and complained of the heat.

'Bad food,' he said.

'Too many people,' I replied. We consoled each other

this way for a few minutes, and then he introduced himself.

'Mack Olive is my name,' he said. I thought it an oddly fitting appellation for an Irishman travelling Greece, and wondered if perhaps one of us had taken too much sun. But it turned out this really was his name, spelled McAulive.

'I'm in a very unusual business,' he replied suggestively when I asked what kept his wife at home. He paused to let his remark sink in, and I was greatly intrigued. What was Mack Olive – a sex therapist, a bookie, the lion tamer in Dublin's only Polish circus?

'I repair vacuum cleaners for Hoover,' he concluded, allowing that he'd done well by it, the business was booming in fact. Someone had to stay home to supervise, so he and his wife took separate holidays.

Mack Olive was hungry and hot. We found a village off the main road and ordered beer and food. He wanted onions. In fact, he was suffering from onion withdrawal.

'I haven't had an onion since I left home,' he said anxiously. 'Can you see if they have some here? There's not an onion to be had anywhere at my hotel.' I asked the woman who was cooking our eggs to give Mack an onion, which she did.

'Very fine,' he said, beaming. 'You take care of the language, and I'll take care of the bill.' This sounded like a good idea, and when we'd finished I helped the woman add up our lunches, adjusting the numbers downward where she had been overgenerous to herself. Mack looked on, understanding nothing but the final figure. He fished out his wad of paper money and handed her a note. She made change.

'What's all these thingamebobs?' he muttered, staring at the hill of coins she'd given him. 'It's ridiculous,' and he dumped the whole pile back in her fist. The woman was amazed. For a moment, while I'd been dickering over the total, she had believed we were quite shrewd. Now she realized we were a couple of rich, foreign kooks.

'You couldn't get a cup of coffee for that price in Dublin,' explained Mack as we walked back to the jeep. 'I don't understand their money. It's heavy enough, but by God it doesn't buy me much at the hotel.'

We cut inland on a dirt road. Mack was tired of the coast. It grew hotter as we moved away from the sea, and he began to puff and perspire. 'I feel the heat here something terrible,' he said. 'Two years ago in Spain I dropped near dead with a heart attack.' We were skirting some fairly lethal precipices along this stretch. I hoped Mack's heart would pump us safely past them. He was a good soul and deserved a holiday somewhere simpler. He didn't much care for the Greek landscape or Greek sun or Greek ruins. Years of squinting down the tubes of ruined vacuum cleaners had, I imagine, altered his perception of the world. What he wanted was somewhere unbroken, shadowy and cool, with a soft humming breeze in the background. Pale and tired, he left me on a main road outside the city and headed for his hotel and another glum night alone.

There were two more days to kill before the weekly steamer would run down to Karpathos. No amount of pestering boat agents could raise another vessel, and they were by now all tired of my questions. A great many people around me were enjoying the luxury for sale on Rhodes, but I wanted only to clear out, so that their harmless pleasures became an annoyance, almost a conspiracy. No other Aegean port had given me this aggrieved, isolated feeling, but it's a sensation that anyone who spends much time on islands must occasionally experience. I felt trapped. The insignificance of my little predicament was brought home when I reread a passage in *Letters from the Levant*. My forebear, having been abandoned on Hydra to await the slow pleasure of a packet master with whom he hoped to leave, wrote the following: 'I had no other alternative than either to hire a small sloop for the remainder of the voyage . . . and thereby run the risk of being plundered and murdered by pirates, or to wait the uncertain chance of a man-of-war. After much cogitation, I resolved to abide by the arrangements which had been made by the packet master; but the prospect before me, and the want of occupation, made me all day little better than disconsolate: to mend matters, the cursed Sirocco had nothing better to do than to blow chagrin and hypochondria into the very marrow of my bones. I ascended to the top of the hills that overlook the town; I counted the windmills on the hills three times; I grew fatigued, and returned to the house. Without books, without amusement, all injuries finished, vexed, disappointed, it seemed as if every object of my existence had suddenly come to an end.'

Such is the gloomy power of islands.

On the boat to Karpathos I counted only eight non-Greeks, a good sign. More interesting, a group of island women stood aloof in traditional costume, the first I'd seen outside the self-conscious masquerade of some enterprising shopkeepers on Rhodes. I didn't know whether the women were Rhodians en route to Crete, where this boat would later stop, or whether they were natives of Karpathos. My bunk was deep in the ship, hot and airless, so I rose at four a.m. and walked the deck in starlight. At four-thirty a caique rose out of the black sea, chug-a-lug-lug-lug, the same dull dependable motor pushing these hardy, all-purpose boats everywhere through the islands. In red-trimmed open caftans and white embroidered blouses the mysterious women crept silently aboard, each gripping several large bundles. Not one of them looked back at the ship as their caique pulled away into another age, swallowed by the murky deep. A cloud of dense black ink hovered over the water a mile away, the north of Karpathos, sparsely populated and difficult to reach. That was where the costumed women were going, and I knew then it was where I would be going too.

12

Karpathos

An hour after the costumed women disembarked, our boat drew alongside the quay at Karpathos' main town. The first fingers of dawn were uncurling, but Pigadia had not yet awakened. Only one harbourfront café flickered with light. I found a table by the water and jotted in my notebook as the morning came on. The Karpathian mountains, faintly illuminated at that hour, their crags in bas-relief against the lingering shadows, seemed the finest mountains I'd seen in Greece. It was exhilarating to escape from Rhodes.

My bag stashed, I'm wandering on the road out of town. Foul air and a snoring Greek in my rat-class cabin allowed me only a couple of hours' sleep. The beach will put everything right. I'm feeling lightheaded. Karpathos seems paradisiacal. Today is the eighteenth of October, a time when all the leaves are turning brown at home, but here the sun burns hot and the mountains still bristle with green. Karpathos, a long thin finger of an island, stretches thirty miles from south to north, with a high mountain spine running up its centre. From Pigadia, a small southern town, and the island capital, one looks across sheltered water to an arm of rough-hewn peaks spearing the sky. Today the mountains are wearing wispy beards of cumulus cloud, and the water is flat and lucid as a window pane. The mountains are still visible on this road, but I've somehow lost the water. From my harbourfront table I could see miles of sandy beach in this direction. There's no one here to direct me now, only silent, dusty fields, a few chickens, occasionally a mule. Then I come to a rotting sign which reads 'Disco-Café.' It points down a dirt path to where I think the sea should be. Perhaps this phantom café will have food. None of the establishments in town had more than dry crusts of bread so early in the day. Perhaps there will be Greek music and dancing. As I say, I'm feeling light-headed. Down the path my body floats, imagining a pleasure palace by the sea. At length the sea does materialize, and by it a little shack with three decrepit tables and some chairs – the disco-café. Once upon a time a radio may have supplied the music, but the radio, like the premises, has rusted out and lies in a sad heap on the reedy sand. Not at all interested in possible customers, the café waiter is fixing his motorcycle. I admire the Greeks for their ingenuity and wily imagination. With a few letters painted on a sign, they transform reality. If next year the new vogue in Europe is elephant waitresses, the disco master will simply repaint his sign to read 'Elephant Waitresses-Café.' And when he is asked where the elephant waitresses are, he will shrug and point up into the mountains, or he will say that the elephant waitresses are having a day off. It won't matter. He knows he is operating the only eatery on the beach and can give it whatever fashionable mask he pleases.

'Have you got tea or coffee?' I enquire. The attendant leaves his motorcycle and reappears in the window of the shack where orders are taken.

'Now,' he begins. 'What would you like?'

'Tea or coffee.'

He shakes his head with apparent regret.

'A little food then,' I suggest.

No food. Not even a dry crust. I'm starting to imagine that this is a contest of wills, that there's a colossal hoard of eggs and beans and tea and coffee back there, if I can only pry it out of him.

'I haven't eaten for two days,' I announce dramatically. 'If you have an egg, or a piece of yesterday's bread, give it to me. Anything. It doesn't matter.'

This, apparently, comes very close to an insult. The attendant raises his voice, calling over the vast silence of sand and water: 'We have no food! Do you understand? We have no food!'

Katalava. Understood. I must be confusing this place with Rhodes, where I thought all the shipping agents were lying to me when they swore there was only one weekly boat to Karpathos. A few more questions gingerly advanced reveals that the one thing for sale here in disco-land is bottled orangeade. I drink one, very cheap, and wander off down the water's edge trying to figure out how the place pays for itself. A thousand bottles a month would clear him about two thousand dollars a year, a bare subsistence wage, but the actual count is probably more like fifty bottles a month. And so on. If he'd given me some food, my mind would have been spared these silly calculations. I hope he owns some olive trees.

Hunger and fatigue put a new perspective on the sea and surrounding mountains. This beach is everyone's dream of a desert island, fine dusty white sand, hot sun, warm embracing water. Karpathos is two hundred miles south of Chios and its climate is notably more tender. When we left Lagada, the water was turning chilly, but here hot springs might be bubbling under the sea. It seems a man could survive indefinitely on this bay with nothing but sun and orangeade, and for a long time I can't think of any reason why I shouldn't try. One other human being has appeared, a young German woman with a hard face and voluptuous body. I know about the body because she has shed all her clothes and is lying spread-eagled twenty yards down from me. The desert island image is complete.

For a mile or so sand coats the shore. I meander along it, in and out of the silky water. This large bay is protected from the open sea and may be where pirate ships used to take refuge. Karpathos is said by some to be a corruption of Arpaktos, meaning robbery island. According to legend, brigand sloops used these shores as a concealed base for hit-and-run raids on passing treasure. That must have been quite recently, as Greek time goes, say within the last five hundred years. Much older ghosts, I see, haunt a reedy wasteland halfway down the beach. Broken marble spindles, so delicate they might shiver after dark, brace their slim lines sunward against the bite of briny air. All around sleep sunken walls and fractured marble blocks. Closer, the spindles become Doric columns and the surrounding detritus a ruined Doric temple. Thin stone plates, elegantly carved, then slowly rubbed by time, lean vulnerably against massive foundation stones. Perhaps this place underwent excavation once, but more likely it was never buried. Variations in grade level with adjoining terrain are negligible. I'm no archaeologist, but the site is almost certainly Doric, because of the style of the columns, and because ancient historians tell us this island was settled in pre-classical times by Dorians from the mainland. Fifty years ago anthropologists confirmed that fragments of the old Doric dialect are still spoken in some Karpathian mountain villages. The Dorians, a northern tribe, penetrated Greece about 1000 B.C.

These stones are entirely abandoned, like rock formations in the sea, without painted signs, without acknowledgement. The amplitude of emptiness here gives the dead room to breathe. They were flesh and blood people, something like me, and I can feel their presence in the ruined shrine. We share the same sense of beauty – a taste for slender columns by a tranquil bay. If that had been my time, an innocent age when men could believe their claims to an island might last forever, I too would have chosen this quiet stretch of sand for my house and altar. Naive the perfection of this temple is, because it stands only a beach's width away from murder and pillage. But perfect nonetheless. 'By no hypothesis within my power of framing,' wrote John Galt, 'can I account for that extraordinary excellence in art which the Greeks so unquestionably attained, except by embracing the notion that the world has its stages of age like man; and supposing that the ancients lived in the youth of the world when all things were more fresh and beautiful than in the state in which we see them.' I like the idea of ancient Greece coming to flower in the youth of the world, even if it is romantic hokum, three thousand years being a mere heartbeat in the life of our planet, a fact not known in my forebear's time. He was certainly on the mark in one sense, though. These columns were raised when cultural memory was young and the burden of man's past relatively small. Recorded history in the Aegean was just beginning. The world, as far as we know, was neither fresher nor more beautiful than it had been for eons, but men's eyes and minds were certainly less cluttered by tangible legacies than they are now. This is what all Doric pillars, simple but elegant, evoke – an unrepeatable time when the manmade world was tabula rasa and an unadorned marble shaft could be lifted toward the sun to embody all of man's fear and pride and humble awe.

Back down past the naked German woman I stroll, looking her way for a kind word, but she's dozing now. In any case, nude bathing is a dangerous sport in this country, and I'm better off not seen with her, or so I tell myself as consolation. According to the newspaper two German skinny dippers were arrested on Crete last week. Uncovered breasts, pudenda and penises are against the law in Greece, and an insult to the morally conservative

Greek temperment. Occasionally, naked tourists are prosecuted.

Sitting shaded again in disco-land, I take another orange drink and wonder if the tavernas in town are open yet for lunch. I'm also wondering how I can get up north to where the beautifully costumed women were going last night. Another man is at the café now, a grey-haired Greek, not drinking orangeade, just sitting. He nods amiably and asks the usual questions – where I'm from and if I have a wife. I give the ritual compliment to his island, saying Karpathos is the most beautiful place I've ever been, which may or may not be true, but sounds plausible when I think of its blood-warm water and white-bearded mountaintops.

'Karpathos has the best climate in the Aegean,' he replies. 'Even better than Crete.' Like my compliment, this boast probably has some truth in it, and some exaggeration too. He's willing enough to talk, so I enquire about the island buses and about Olimpos, the northern village where I hope to stay.

'Yes, we have buses,' he says. 'But not to Olimpos. The road through the mountains is very bad. You must hire a truck. Or take the boat up to Diaphani. Olimpos is only half an hour from there.' He's interested in my plans. We chat a bit, and then he invites me home for coffee. Yiorgo his name is, and he is the owner of this bizarre little beachside café, with a house and garden immediately behind. He picks a handful of ripe pomegranates for me, and then we sit in the kitchen. I was curious to see the inside of a Karpathian house, but it's no different from those I've seen on islands farther north: small, spare rooms with functional furniture.

Yiorgo deftly steers the discussion around to religion while his wife boils water and spoons out coffee. He asks me what denomination I am and whether I go to church.

There is nothing unusual about these questions. God, family, food and money are endlessly interesting to the Greeks, though after a few minutes I sense that this man is more fervent in his beliefs than most. He is running down the system, by which I take him to mean the Orthodox Church. *To sisteima*, he keeps saying, the system is bad. God is good. The Bible is right. What's wrong is *to sisteima*.

'I know the system,' he continues. 'The Pappas get rich. Money is all they want. But that is not what the gospels preach.' Unfortunately I understand almost every word of this boring patter. Since coming to Greece I've heard so much God-talk that most of the everyday expressions connected with church, bible and religious morality are familiar. But I'm incredulous when he arrives at his punch line.

'I used to be Orthodox. Now I'm a Jehovah's Witness.'

There are a small number of Roman Catholics in this country, a legacy from the Venetian and Genoese periods, but the vast majority of Greeks are Orthodox. Yiorgo is the first dissenter I've come across, and I tell him so.

'But we are many,' he says defensively. 'Three thousand Jehovah's Witnesses in all of Greece. And every year more.'

I can't stop him now. He's off and running, firing questions at me and declaiming from two ominous-sounding Witness textbooks. I'm trying to deflate the gloomy prayer-meetng atmosphere with asides about how none of this really matters, it's all the same to me, we'll be dead soon anyway, I never go to church, and so on, but he has a smooth comeback for every mockery. No, we won't be dead soon. If we follow God's law, we'll live forever.

'I don't want to live forever.'

'Do you like the sea, the sun, the garden outside my house?'

'Yes. Of course. Very nice garden.'

'Then you want to live forever.'

The conversation follows this whacky vein for an hour or so. Then, after much proselytizing, he reflects, 'It's a pity you don't read Greek. You could take a day from your time on Karpathos and read my theology books.'

'No!' I shout, surprising both of us. For a while this exchange had been mildly entertaining. I was interested to see how far I could go in Greek – much too far, obviously. 'I don't read such books,' I shout again, and then, switching to English: 'I wouldn't read such books if they were the last printed pages on earth. They're deadly books written by bores.' Yiorgo calmly reminds me he doesn't speak my language.

I'm about to make my getaway at this point when a young woman walks in, the daughter. Home on holiday for a few weeks, she lives in Canada, and is a Jehovah's Witness too. She'll explain the whole thing to me once more in English, says Yiorgo, and then I'll see his point. Still no one offers any food. Yiorgo's is indeed a merciless God. In the end I duck out quite abruptly, because that is the only way.

By the time I get back to town, it's afternoon, lunch has come and gone, and the tavernas are closed again. The sun, the sleepless night, the empty stomach, fire and brimstone at the disco-café, the blood-warm sea and bluebeard mountains, all leave me game and exuberant and a little shaky too. Pigadia fed and slumbering, the sun a multitude of brilliant spears hurled on the empty pavement, this must be an hour when Karpathos yields up its most elusive, ghostly dreams. Staring out to sea, I'll take whatever comes, as long as it happens here and now with flesh and blood, as long as I needn't bide my time hoping to live forever.

★   ★   ★

Sailing up the Karpathian coast in daylight, a man can admire its rugged mountains falling sharply into the sea. Another clear, hot day it is, with our ship's wash the only furrow in an otherwise impassive channel. The stillness of it, and the remoteness of this route brings to mind a romantic passage from my ancestor's book: 'The Corsair's shot cut some of our rigging, but in the end she was beaten off and went away, crawling with her oars along the smooth sea, like a centipede on a plate of glass.' That repelled pirate ship retreating over calm waters, the lone caterpillar sculling across an endless liquid sheet, serves now to symbolize all wind-powered vessels and the vast expanse of slow time they were once given to plough.

A little of that unhurried, pre-steam pace survives on this Karpathian launch, not in the mode of propulsion, but in some of the passengers. A group of the costumed women are here, moving on deck gravely and deliberately, not at all skittish, not at all coy. They meet each curious glance with a hard, unflinching stare, taking good time over the eyes of a stranger. I suspect they dismiss me as one who will not stay long, an object that passes, like driftwood on the waves, but I can't really tell what they might be thinking. Dress and language; the way we hold our faces; our separate purposes for this trip; their unfathomable sense of yesterday, today and tomorrow; all this divides us and shuts me out. A tribe apart they are, the people of Olimpos, even on their own island. In the main port yesterday two proudly costumed women strode past my table, and I asked the café waiter why some natives hold to traditional dress here, while others have adopted the modern style.

'You mean the women?' he gestured. 'They are from the north, down to visit relatives. No one from Pigadia wears the old clothes now.' Olimpos, he added, remains the only village on Karpathos where traditional dress is still routinely worn. The others gave it up generations ago. And it is in Olimpos where remnants of the Doric dialect are still spoken.

When we reach Diaphani, the small northern port, a caique putters out to meet us, and we clamber aboard, a few other travellers come for the day, half a dozen costumed women, two local men, three goats, a pig tied in a sack, and some hens. The villagers stake out positions well away from the three goat rumps, and I am signed to do the same, which turns out to be a wise move. One rump shits buckets on the crowded deck as soon as we cast off. The caique master curses it loudly.

On shore are a handful of houses, a canteen and a small hotel – nothing of interest. Diaphani was built less than a hundred years ago as a maritime outlet for Olimpos. Like many twin villages in Greece, one inland and one on the sea, these two form a single community, even though Olimpos is several miles away and until recently could be reached only by mule. In fact, the inland village lies closer to the opposite coast according to my map, beyond a range of high hills. The far side of this island must run with extraordinarily treacherous waters for the port to have been built over here.

At the crossroads in town a pick-up truck is waiting. The driver slaps three boards across the back and we crowd on to them, baggage and small animals underneath. The goats will walk. I'm curious to know what the fare will be for this improvised bus. Beside me a man shrugs. 'Whatever it costs,' he says sadly, 'we will pay.'

It's a twenty-minute ride up through rough country. The motor road, shouts my bouncing bench mate, is only a few years old. He points to a path which touches our track from time to time, and says it's the donkey trail everyone used to travel.

'It's shorter,' he adds. 'But a donkey has no engine.'

We turn a high bend and the village swings into view cinematically, a cubist mantle on the jagged mountain ridge, as if a giant had spilled his sack of blocks here, and some were impaled on the pinnacle while others slid partway down. The driver halts us and steps out into the dust.

'*Photografies*,' he announces. Two obedient tourists climb down and snap some pictures.

The road arcs in a long, lazy crescent and then we reach a gravel terrace where Olimpos' few vehicles are parked. Even if the village lanes were wide enough for cars, which they aren't, it would still be impossible to drive past this gravel. All public passageways here are stepped up and down the mountain.

Weighing each piece of baggage on an invisible scale somewhere behind his eyes, the driver collects our money. Apparently the mechanism is foolproof – no one complains. He tells me of a house where I can get good food and lodging, and points into the middle of the spilled cubes. On the way there the aroma of cooking bread tickles my nose.

'Where is the bakery?' I ask the first villager who passes, leading a mule.

'The bakery?' he repeats, evidently astonished, as if I'd asked for the local used car dealer. But then he shrugs, and points up a rocky incline where I see two women stoking an outdoor fire. It seems a primitive and undersized bakery even for this small village. I climb up and nod to the women, and they stare back quizzically.

'I want to buy some bread.'

'Buy bread? Buy bread?' they cackle, looking at each other puzzled. 'You can't buy bread here,' and one faces me reproachfully, but also with apology in her eyes. I've blundered, I realize suddenly, because of my sloppy Greek. I asked where the *fournos* was, meaning bakery, but *fournos* also means household oven. These two are cooking bread for their own families. Olimpos, of course, has no bakery. It's too small. Embarrassed, the women insist on giving away chunks of their few fresh loaves to me and the other travellers who have followed me up this path. I ask the others to take only a polite mouthful. The women are thin and drawn and evidently poor, and though their hospitality must be accepted, it's obvious we're imposing on scant resources. The village could offer no better welcome than these crusts of bread so freely shared. Deep brown, thick, chewy, and redolent of charred wood, it's the best loaf I've tasted in Greece.

Evening. The other tourists have left. Heavy with cash, they hired a truck and driver to make a run from Pigadia up through the mountains to fetch them. They were uneasy about spending a night here.

I don't know what to make of Olimpos. We generally believe that tightly knit villages like this where traditional costume is worn and ancient custom still observed survive only in remote parts of Africa, Asia and South America, but this one is in Europe, only a few hours by sea from the fleshpot of Rhodes with its international yachting set and casino dandies. As far as I'm aware, no other such village exists in these islands, though several are said to flourish in the mountains near Albania. Up there traditional weaving is still a prosperous industry. Olimpos enjoys no such strong economic base. The people here scratch a living from the land, as they have since the Dorians set foot on these slopes between two and three thousand years ago. A few families fish from the lower port. Whatever cash circulates in the village comes from a handful of tourists in the summer, from pensions, and from men who send wages home from abroad.

Two cafés operate near the pinnacle. Across from the

church sits the one I'm in, drinking beer with a local carpenter.

'According to history,' the carpenter declaims, 'eighty families originally moved here, forming Olimpos from several smaller villages. That was five hundred years ago. They wanted to be together because of the danger of pirates. When they built the houses, they made them all of grey stone, like the mountain, so no one would know they were here.' Most of the village, I discovered on my walk earlier, clings to the leeward side of the mountain, entirely concealed from the sea. This must be where the first houses were built, out of sight of any marauders. I also discovered why the local port was built at Diaphani and not over on this closer coast. Olimpos is, in fact, a seaside village, but the cliffs on the seaward side fall dramatically almost half a mile before they reach the water. To cut a stable pathway in that sheer rockface must have been judged impossible.

I ask the carpenter why only the women here wear traditional dress. He replies that some of the men have gone away to America and West Germany and for two generations now have brought home a taste for *rouha moderna*, modern clothes. But about the women he says this: 'Wherever they go, our women wear the clothes of Olimpos. When they go to the southern villages to work or put their children in high school, of course, they keep the village costume, but even when they go to Athens, even if they live in Athens for many years, they always do the same.' He adds that sometimes in Athens the women are mocked for their old-fashioned ways.

The amicable carpenter buys me another drink and we talk on. He's one of the few men here who have been able to work close to home, either in the village, or in the south of Karpathos, or on the little island of Cassos nearby. He's never been abroad and never been to Athens.

In fact, he's never been anywhere but Karpathos and Cassos, not even to Rhodes or Crete, both of which are within an easy day's sail. I think I can understand a man's reluctance to go away from Olimpos. Unless he badly needed work, anywhere else would seem shallow and deflating.

It's growing late. The café owner has ignited his powerful gas lamp. Olimpos is still without electricity, one of the few such villages left in Greece. When I walk out into the street and beyond the light pool at the café door, darkness traps me, as if I'd fallen down a well. We don't know what darkness is anymore. Tonight the sky is overcast, and there are no street lights. Blind, I have no idea how to get back to my pension, so I strike some matches and grope down to the next level of pathways where the village store, a single cramped room about ten feet by eight, proffers a dim gas flame. The storekeeper tries to describe my route through the laddered laneways, then gives up and sends her daughter, with a battery-powered torch, as a guide.

At the pension, three Cretan workmen are eating together. The itinerant photographer, whom I met earlier in the day, is sitting alone. He beckons me to join him and buys the drinks. A strange life this one leads. His woman and children stay in Athens while he travels by himself ten months of the year taking family portraits in small island villages. We had such peripatetic cameramen in North America in the last century. He says he makes not a bad living, as long as he moves quickly and goes to the right places. Some villages, regardless of their wealth, are better than others. Olimpos, he confides in a low voice, is very good.

We eat fresh fish, caught by the pension keeper's husband, who works a boat out of Diaphani. The Cretans and the photographer retire, though it's not late. People here sleep and rise with the sun. Looking out from this balcony into the inky night below, I can see two pinpoints of burning gas, nothing more. Every house is alone in a deep pool of darkness, dreaming neo-Dorian dreams, or so I imagine. It's all coming to an end. The Cretan workmen are bringing in power lines from a supply station down south. By next summer when the tourists come – there are a few tourists now every year – the village will be electrified. For a century Olimpos has lingered peacefully in the dark. By coincidence, it was a hundred years ago today that Thomas Edison tested his first effective lightbulb. Now the hot wires are finally reaching this isolated mountain where they will switch on televisions, stoves, and above all, lightbulbs, and switch off centuries of slow, traditional time. Television will, I'm sure, eliminate the ancient costume within a generation or two. Life will be easier, giving these people the comfort they deserve, and that is good, but I feel sad nonetheless here at the edge of this time zone, possibly the last foreigner to see Olimpos as it was first conceived. Lighting a kerosene lamp, I imagine myself the last traveller in old Greece, the last of a long line which included my literary ancestor and flocks of unknown wanderers, poets, lords and lackeys, boring antiquarians, scoundrels on the lam, amateur anthropologists, deadbeat nymphs and satyrs, and assorted burnt-out cases, all of whom came searching for and often found another look at life, a second chance, an inspiration or a dream. I regret this line coming to an end, though of course, there is a new line of electronic travellers long since begun. They see differently, and sometimes wonderfully, but they will never see the unhurried, proud bearing of these self-reliant people who shape all thought and action from a slow, unwired mountain and break their daily darkness with the sun.

★   ★   ★

Wandering through the laneways next morning, I see many women, but only a scattering of men, mostly old. A fair number of houses are closed and empty. Everyone I speak with says the same. *Fevgoun ta pathia*. The children are leaving. *Efygan*. They have left. These are mostly older women speaking, so by children they mean anyone under forty. The population here is steadily thinning. Many men are working abroad and many families have moved to Athens. They keep their houses and come back here when they can, usually for a holiday in the summer.

An old woman asks if I can fix her battery-powered radio. I say no, that I haven't the skill, and she nods disappointedly, moving back inside. How slow-witted of me. The women here are direct and friendly, but no Greek female can invite a strange man into her house, not unless she is doing an errand. She might have been inviting me for coffee, as it were. In any case, I could have seen inside her dwelling.

Another old woman is watching her granddaughter bake bread. I pause to watch them. The grandmother looks up.

'Where is your wife?' she shrieks, as if she'd known me for years. I've never seen her before.

'My wife is in France,' I reply.

'You should have brought her,' she shouts, shaking her head.

Other women pass carrying large sacks of flour, heavy cylinders of propane, or cement blocks. They cart these burdens up and down the stepped pathways as if they were carrying straw handbags. As strong as their mules these women are. I haven't seen a village with such lovely women anywhere else in the islands. Their features are generally fine, and life on the mountain leaves them sinewy and nimble.

Far below the houses on the inland side of the peak

winds a narrow gully, sown with a thin seam of green. I descend slowly, through levels of the town, and then on to raw gravel and shale, until reaching the gully floor. A woman from the village might go up and down this steep declivity two or three times a day, carrying bundles on her back. Once will be plenty for me. At bottom runs a generous stream, with miniature stone aqueducts rerouting rivulets into gardens on either side. There are chapels in the village, dozens of them, and chapels down here too, whitewashed, with small crosses set on the peak above the door. I sit on the steps of one and watch a woman tend her garden. She has hoisted her black smock and fastened it under her belt, and has done the same with her pale undersmock, and stands now in sheer white culottes tucked into the hardy full length boots which are still made in the village by two old cobblers. She is magnificently dressed and must know it; else why would she and all the others continue to make and wear this complex garb? Or does it become, after two thousand years, mere second nature, almost instinctual, like a parrot's plumage? It's true that these women escape the inner curse of our inner age – anxious self-doubt mixed with manic self-esteem, but no, they are not like dumb unthinking birds dressed in nature's colourful plumage, not at all. They are perfectly aware of who they are and what distinctions they possess. Their imposing confidence shows that. They *know*, with absolute certainty and immoveable pride, and because they know, it's unnecessary for them to question the ways of this mountain realm, and unlikely that they covet the ragtag life outside. For them, the centre holds here, and beyond these peaks mere anarchy tips the world.

The sun sinks, and I head back to the pension while dusk is still flickering. Other people are walking home too. The itinerant photographer has left, so the Cretan construction workers invite me to their table along with many bottles of wine. They've ordered hare stew tonight and insist that I partake. A hard-living crew they are, away from their families in Crete for months at a time, and much given to booze and impassioned talk. Their conversation touches on a wide range of subjects – politics, history, literature and, as always, money. One of them has read a Kazantzakis novel and says he's the best writer who ever lived. Well, maybe not the best. Maybe there are better writers he hasn't heard of. But the best writer in Greece! No doubt about that!

'The Pappas,' I interject, 'didn't like Kazantzakis.'

'Enough,' commands Spiro, the feisty-eyed one. 'Leave it. We mustn't say such things. There might be trouble.' He's serious. Again, here is the Greek fear of unseen malevolent authority. But they aren't mealymouthed, these Cretans, not at all cringing. They have strong opinions and express them forcefully. Spiro, when he wants to emphasize his contempt for the imaginary opposition, grabs his knife and makes a slashing motion across his wrist.

'I'd cut his hand off,' he snorts. He's very convincing. When he tells the story of an American soldier on Crete who ripped up the Greek flag one drunken night, he sweeps his blade across his own throat and growls: 'That's what I'd have done to him if I'd been there.' Spiro's threats are partly good drama, but I wouldn't want to call his bluff. The Cretan reputation for wild tempers and blood-lust is well founded in history. They also enjoy a special reputation for courtesy and hospitality, and Spiro shows me this side too. In the darting shadows of our gas lamp his face fairly crackles with glee when he hears I'll be in Greece a while longer.

'Stay, *Yiorgo*,' he coaxes. 'Stay another month and when my work is finished we'll go to Crete together. You'll be

my guest.' So far away from everything I know, under a
flickering lamp on this dark Greek summit, it does seem
possible that I'll stay a month or two, or even more,
drinking heady wine by night with the fiery Cretans, and
watching by day the proud women of Olimpos run up
and down the mountain building and rebuilding their
world.

Down in Pigadia, this is my last night on the island. I feel
better now, almost recovered. Food poisoning or bad
water hit me in Olimpos, my body erupting at both ends.
It seemed imperative to leave, though I regret it now.
Then again, I would have regretted leaving any time,
regardless of the circumstances. Olimpos was like no
other place in these islands.

The local pick-up truck happened to be making a run
down south through the mountains yesterday, so I was
able to catch a lift. A spectacular rocky ride it was along
the central ridge of skinny Karpathos, the sea visible on
both sides through lush stands of pine. Some women from
the village accompanied us part way. The last one to leave
the truck looked to be about sixty-five, and we dropped
her several miles from home. She had another half mile to
travel on foot before she would reach her olive grove on a
little plateau hundreds of yards below near the sea. Sometime before sunset she would walk home alone. It's far
from safe, this rugged mountain life. Another old woman
had disappeared in the hills the week before, and still had
not been found.

Pigadia, where I'm staying tonight, is another world
after Olimpos, though not much closer to home for me.
There is still a feeling of remoteness here, and an ambience
of undiluted Greekness. The café owner's son is cleaning
tabletops. His friend, who's downed many shots of ouzo,
sits watching him and joking.

'This is how you're going to spend your years?' he

mocks good-naturedly. 'Wiping tables for the rest of your life?'

The working one, mildly annoyed, returns the challenge. 'Yes. And you, what are you going to do with your life? Sit and watch me wipe?'

The drunken one falls silent for a moment and reflects. 'No,' he answers deliberately, and he seems half-serious now. 'No – I am going to be a *logotechnis*,' which translates literally in English as word artist. There are other Greek terms for journalist and for writer. *Logotechnis* is a term reserved for great literary practitioners, generally those who devote themselves to poetry or fiction. The owner's son stops wiping and pretends to be suitably impressed.

'Really?' he says. 'Good luck to you then,' and he laughs at the improbability of it. The exchange intrigues me. I could never have heard anything like it at home. At home the drunken one, casting about for an impossibly lofty aspiration, would have fastened on being a millionaire, perhaps a film star or sports hero, or perhaps a nuclear physicist. Here the impossible dream is to be a word artist. I admire the Greek scheme of things.

A last meal taken in one of the smoky harbourfront tavernas. Karpathos ends well. The island is known for its music, and finally in this steaming eatery a local man is playing the three-stringed lyra. He's plucking wonderful melodies for us, a strange mix of Country-and-Western fiddle songs and the inscrutable tones of the Indian sitar. It's more repetitive and haunting than our fiddle music, more Eastern, but also jaunty and foot-tappable. We're all clapping him on as we eat fish and drink retsina. It's a good way to leave.

13

The Ghosts of Kato Zakro

Crete is where the Aegean begins geographically and where all of Greece began historically, sometime around 3000 B.C. Five months ago I wasn't sure I'd make it here, but this week when I saw the island rising so close to Karpathos on the map, I knew I'd be stopping for a look. This is where Europe crawled from the cave to build its first palaces and shape its first elegant pots. A traveller should see those palaces, if only some small corner of one or two. It would take months, maybe years, to traverse in detail the whole island, 140 miles long and from 8 to 38 miles wide. Heading for Mykonos on a final Greek errand, I didn't have anything like that much time. But the ship out of Karpathos would touch at two Cretan ports, so I decided to choose one and spend a few days exploring.

I'm closer to one of those palaces now. From Siteia, the island's easternmost deep-water harbour, I've taken a bus to this fork at Palaiokastro. The fork will lead me to a romantic sounding village – Kato Zakro – if I have any luck. No bus travels the rough route here, so I'll go with my thumb or not at all. It's difficult to reach, though apparently worth the trouble. Crete's most recently excavated Minoan ruin, the Palace of Kato Zakro, lies at the end of this road on a little plain by the sea. I'm hoping for a farmer or fisherman with one of the three-wheeled trucks many Greeks own, but so far there have been no wheels at all, and I've been standing here for over an hour. The eastern coast must be sparsely populated.

I'm thinking of giving up when a rusty van rolls out of

town along my prong of the fork. From a distance I saw it stop in the plateia of Palaiokastro, and it seemed to me that many people got out to stretch and buy some bottles, like twenty clowns staggering from a phone booth. I don't suppose they have room for an extra passenger, but they do stop, and invite me in, and I'm sufficiently intrigued that I don't ask where they're going. Wherever it is, I'll come along for the ride.

There aren't twenty people inside, only seven, and making for the end of the road. We will see the palace. Most of them are Australian, staying together in a rented villa outside Siteia. Lloyd, the driver, is from Canada. It's loose and easy inside the van. Hair down to his shoulders, Lloyd is flipping one cassette after another on to the tape deck, spinning through the Minoan landscape to hammer-drum rhythms, the likes of Fleetwood Mac and Meatball. Lloyd's electronic music separates us from the island, holds us in our mobile Western world, so that I have the impression of watching a spectacular travel film on Cretan countryside unwinding in my corner of the window. More than anything it is magnitude that holds the eye here. The mountains are fuller and higher, the foothills less cramped, the valleys broader than the ones I've travelled through all summer. Crete is all the other Aegean islands writ large.

Our parade is hungry, so we stop at Zakro, the upper twin village of Kato Zakro, and troup into a taverna. The owner, Manoli by name, thinks us quite outlandish. After bringing the food, he sits down to talk, some sentences in broken English, some in Greek.

'You,' he says, singling me out. 'You smoke hashish, yes? I see it in the eyes,' and he grins an enormous friendly grin, as if he's hoping to score some dope. They must have had the complete cross-section of foreign youth pass through this town in recent years.

'No,' I reply. 'I've had food poisoning.' He doesn't understand.

'All you people,' he continues jovially, 'you all make a big needle and put the heroin, yes?' With an imaginary syringe he jabs his thick arm. 'Very good, yes?' Everyone protests, but I have a better idea now of the impression we're making. Nine or ten years ago, at the tail end of the disaffected sixties, Crete was invaded by a mob of counter-culture diehards from America and northern Europe. They came to live cheaply in good weather, to do drugs, loll under the sun, and copulate in whatever combinations pleased them on the open sand. The Cretans were horrified, and eventually cleaned out any beaches and caves where communes-in-exile had taken root. I think Manoli associates us with those swept-away libertines. But he finds our oddness entertaining, and insists on serving a free round of coffee and fiery raki before we go.

Five more miles it is to Kato Zakro. The road is deteriorating, narrow and jagged, and the landscape is going bald. A savage split opens the rock beside our dirt track and widens as we descend to the sea. The Valley of the Dead this gorge is called. When we stop and look over the precipice, I understand why. Sucking at our feet yawns a deep, dry canyon, a predatory orifice of thirsty air, planted with spearhead rocks. The only way down is to slip and plummet. There's no way back up.

Kato Zakro at first sight suggests a peaceful, pre-human place, silent, Paleozoic, sublime. We clear the natural rockwall which encloses this little plain, and then wind steeply down to sea level. Some signs of human life appear, not many. A few low buildings crouch by the water, and parts of the plain are cultivated. The lush green leaves turn out to be banana fronds, and they perfectly suit the mood of this place: protected and benign. There ought to be a pair of dinosaurs hidden in those leaves, feeding on the ripening fruit. But I suppose all local dinosaurs fled into the sea when roadbuilders first swaggered over the enclosing rockwall. Once upon a time, before the makeshift road, this little plain could be reached only by able hikers and boats.

A cold breeze sweeps the entire pebble beach. If there were any holidayers at Kato Zakro this year, they've gone. We don't see anyone at all, not until a man appears along the water's edge carrying a shot gun.

'Birds?' I enquire.

'Greek?' he asks in return, apparently pleased to see us, and even more pleased when we say we're foreigners. He leads the way to his taverna, one of only half a dozen buildings down here, and insists we sit as his guests for a round of raki. Expansiveness, it seems, runs in the clan. Manoli, our jolly taverna keeper in upper Zakro, is this man's brother.

The Palace of Zakro would be a disappointing ruin except that our new friend agrees to guide us through. All that remains are ankle-high footings, mere outlines of the ancient rooms, but Manoli's brother, who was employed on the initial dig here in 1962 and for several summers thereafter, probably knows the palace as well as anyone. From the footings he conjures rooms, and from dead brush, Minoans. We found drinking vessels in this dirt, he explains; and in that room, coins. Here the double axes and over there charred elephant tusks. He shows us what are said to be the royal chamber, the bath room, the kitchen and the archives. Using a bizarre mixture of Greek and French and Italian, he rebuilds the Palace for us, and furnishes it too, so that it is possible to catch a fleeting ghostly glimpse of the people we call Minoan who lived on this hideaway plain until about 1500 B.C. I prefer to think of them building the walls rather than fleeing them as the settlement fell. They stood here, as we do, their first stones laid, trying to imagine, as we do, the effect of the finished Palace.

Back up and over the rockwall in the dying light we go, eyes outside on shadowy Minoans dancing to the Rolling Stones. There does seem to be an uneasy link tonight between Lloyd's electronic music and the ghosts of Kato Zakro. Both speak to our sense of dangerous ritual, our sense of doom, our fear of overwhelming power and decay. No one knows what happened to the Minoans on Crete, though theories abound. Minoan culture is thought by some to have been swept away by a devastating natural disaster, a tidal wave and ash storm resulting from the eruption of Santorini, a volcanic island to the north. Others claim the Minoans were victims of their own decadence, that they collapsed in the face of Mycenean assaults from the mainland. No one knows. Lloyd's wailing music rides the same currents of lust and wonderment and dread that carry us when we think of the fate of these ancient people and their palaces, and also when we think of our own finality. What will happen? How do we end?

Walking from the Australians' villa into town, five dark miles, I'm not entirely free of the ghosts of Kato Zakro. Crashing waves on one side, spooky shadows of jagged Crete on the other, the clouded moon my only light, I'm tailed by prehistoric phantoms, poisonous reptiles and man-eating wolves, the ineluctable Minoan apocalypse that threatens to overtake each one of us in the dead of night. This is how it happens, a man alone on a dark road, a sudden clawing at the leg, pulling, pulling, lungs sucking for air, a limp body spread on the rocks at dawn. What in hell is a man doing out here at two o'clock wandering in an unknown world? Some Greeks who pass in their car must be asking the same question. They stop and offer a lift, four hearty souls on their way home from drinking in a Cretan taverna. The ghosts of Kato Zakro are gone.

In Greece the cheapest hotels always take the grandest names. I'm in Iraklion, Crete's largest city, staying at the Palladium. There is no delicate way to describe the odour of this establishment. It smells of shit, in the halls, the common toilets, the airless rooms, shit everywhere. It's very cheap, of course. And very cold. November has come. I went to the owner and asked for blankets. 'Are there no blankets on your bed?' he demanded. Remembering two damp, shirt-thin rags upstairs, I said there were. *Then you have blankets*, he enunciated clearly, as if talking to a moron, a moron who tended to forget everything but the last three words. *You have blankets*. That was the end of it. He turned and waved me off.

Iraklion, badly damaged during the last war, resembles the ugliest parts of modern Athens, sprawling acres of concrete block apartment towers staggered among dusty open lots – in short, a giant construction site. People come, as I have, for specific attractions: the Palace of Knossos, the archaeological museum, the Lasithi Plateau an hour's drive into the mountains. Even a visitor with no antiquarian interests whatever must feel some enthusiasm for the archaeological museum's collection. The elegant urns and rhytons, some of the heraldic armour and statuary, the ornamented sarcophagi and delicate little cups, all would command attention if they had been cast yesterday, even without the mystery of three and a half thousand years. What else can be said? Go. The eye must see them.

Knossos is less interesting to the eye than the objects taken from it and displayed in the museum, but no less interesting to the mind. Knossos remains a puzzle. Sir Arthur Evans, who excavated the site early in this century, identified it as the royal palace of a people he called Minoan, after the legendary Cretan King Minos. It was the Bull of Minos that Evans found, or thought he found, decorating many of his unearthed artifacts. The Minoans, however, most scholars now believe were the elusive Keftiu people who apparently were familiar to the ancient Egyptians. Painted images of the Keftiu-Cretans have been found in the pyramids. On the basis of this connection and much other evidence, the German geologist Hans Wunderlich put forward some years ago the thesis that Knossos was not a palace at all, but a gargantuan mortuary, centre of an ancient Cretan cult of the dead somewhat similar to the Egyptian cult. His argument is compelling. Perhaps he is right, perhaps wrong. At the very least he challenges us to examine Knossos and Evans' theatrical restorations there with a critical eye. Wunderlich's theories invest the site with otherworldly wraiths, ghostly embalmers, grave robbers and ghouls; and it is in such company that Knossos should be seen. Rebuilding the great walls and intricate web of rooms in my mind's eye, I stalked the faintly lit, labyrinthine corridors increasingly persuaded that the rituals of death were enacted here, that this was where mourners sang and not where royals feasted. King's mansion or House of the Dead? It is uncertainty about this place which leaves us room to peer and feel afraid, and it is morbid fear which pulls the unknown Keftiu closer, seeping through the giant urns, drawing near enough to change your living shadow to a corpse.

There are many other Minoan sites on Crete, several of them palaces or towns, and there are many other modern settlements, most, it is said, more attractive than Iraklion. I explored the well preserved Minoan town of Gournia one sunny afternoon, visited green Lasithi another, and walked through the winsomely bedraggled medieval town of Rethymnon, but the longer I stay on the island, the more I feel that Crete cannot really be touched in a week or two. Crete demands months, or years, or perhaps a lifetime. There is a bigness to it, and a variety, which overshadow the other islands. I don't wish them to be overshadowed in memory, at least not yet. So I'm moving on. The inter-island boats have been taken in for winter, but a year-round ship to Athens sails this evening. From there I'll catch a run out to Mykonos.

Yesterday, after looking at Nikos Kazantzakis' preserved study in the historical museum, I went searching for his grave. The study was a vacuous place, a novelist's desk, a chair, his framed photograph, shelves of dog-eared books, but nothing of the man's titanic spirit. The grave, by contrast, possesses a measure of dignity and conveys a mood of triumph. Because of his feud with Orthodoxy, the Greek Church would not allow Kazantzakis to be buried in consecrated ground. Interred alone on a medieval wall overlooking the city, he has been given a place of honour by his fellow islanders. The simple wooden cross stands centred in an ample square plot enclosed by bougainvillea. No name marks this grave, no dates, only an inscription taken from his writing and carved on stone: 'I hope for nothing. I fear nothing. I am free.' It is an eloquent epitaph for a man who chose to write and speak whatever he wanted in spite of often contrary pressures from those in authority. High on unconsecrated ground, his final words escape the repressive clutches of priests and politicians, of all those fearful, mean-minded men who would smother any stirring of dissent. There is a sameness of mind in Greece, perhaps characteristic of any tightly knit, traditional culture, which I have found cloying. This forceful call to independence at Kazantzakis' tomb left me exuberant, reminding as it does that simple, clear words and the resolve to use them can break the bonds of hundreds of years, and set one imprisoned man free.

My southern circuit finishes in a taverna near the boat to Athens. They have produced another piece of miserably shrivelled chicken, the same piece of shrunken, disabled bird I've been eating in island tavernas since May. Once I counted – four small bites exactly. But the chicken is cheap and a man must feed on something. It occurs to me as I pull a pubic hair out of my lemonade and swat the swarm of flies I'm always brushing away in these places, not to mention the mangy cats, that Greek tavernas are neither elegant nor clean. The same thought has passed through my mind many times before, sometimes a troubling thought, sometimes oddly invigorating, but either way no substitute for more chicken. There is always other food available, though not the variety a patron of Greek restaurants abroad might expect. Dishes like moussaka and roast lamb are rare in the islands, except at expensive tavernas in a well travelled centre like Rhodes. Fish is surprisingly scarce, the sad result of an overfished and polluted sea. Usually I ask for a filler of cheese to follow my ragged chicken, and often it's only this last plate which has any real feeling of food. But what food! Feta cheese after tasteless chicken is like good red wine after rancid water. Though always similar in appearance – a rectangular white slice on a simple white dish – it offers an endless variety of taste. Some feta is salty; some hard, pungent and crumbly; some soft, moist and chewy; some delicate, fit for a gentle wine; some clamorous and forceful, tasting of the dung-strewn hills; but always hearty nourishment, a slice of Greece itself. When all else fails, when the cheap hotel room with filth in every crack drives you out, when the sixth ticket agent claims to know nothing about your boat, when you stand with your thumb out for hours and no one stops, then this matchless slab of white provender, hard white as the houses on Paros or soft white as an August cloud, this simple goat's milk tablet will wipe the curse from your mouth and replenish your love for this land.

15

The House of the Russian Consul

Even if I didn't have business on Mykonos, I would have
come here, although without great enthusiasm. It is
reputed to be the most architecturally vivid of Cycladic
towns, but also the one most spoiled by tourism. Daily
cruise ships stop at this island, and then at Rhodes and
Santorini. So many transient visitors over the past two
decades have left their mark: street upon street of souvenir
shops, expensive clothing salons, and jewellery boutiques.
Like Rhodes, Mykonos has done very well from the
tourist trade, and like Rhodes, it has sacrificed a measure
of its authenticity.

Just the same, this town's intricate medieval plan pleases
the eye and mind. Whiter than Paros, with more complex
turning and tunnelling, Mykonos seems a kind of manmade sugar-coated grotto, where elves and griffins ought
to live. The streets twist every which way, a design meant
to confuse marauding pirates, and a visitor loses his
bearings still. Each street has a chapel, and some have two
or three. 'The number of churches,' wrote John Galt, 'is
so incredible that I shall not attempt to form an estimate
of it. . . . Till very lately, it was the practice of the sailors
and shipowners, on escaping from any extraordinary
danger, to build a church in testimony of their gratitude
to the saint whose aid they had implored.'

My ancestor came to Mykonos for the same reason he
had visited Hydra two months before, to investigate the
port as a possible base for the trading enterprise he
envisioned. There is an interesting sidelight to these

excursions. At one point he encountered the agent of the
Earl of Elgin, one Signore Luseri, who was in possession
of what we now call the Elgin Marbles. The statuary,
packed and ready for freighting to England, was being
held at the port of Piraeus in lieu of payment. Luseri had
been unable to settle his bills due for handling, and turned
to Galt for advice. My ancestor agreed to take responsibility for the marbles and to have them delivered to Malta,
on the understanding that if the shipping costs were
charged against his account, the booty would be his.
Discretion barred this anecdote from the travel book, but
it appeared later (1833) in his autobiography. 'Here was a
chance,' he wrote, 'of the most exquisite relics of art in
the world becoming mine, and a speculation by the sale of
them in London that would realize a fortune. The temptation was too great.' He wrote his Maltese agents
instructing them to pay the bills, and had the cargo
shipped to Hydra where it was given the protection of a
man-of-war for the more exposed journey to Malta. 'But
on [the boat's] arrival there, the agent for the Earl paid the
bills, and my patriotic cupidity was frustrated. It should
be confessed that I had a suspicion of this coming to pass.'
It's a little disappointing that the Earl stole Galt's thunder,
and plunder, so early in the tale, but I'm not sorry the
marbles bear Elgin's rather than my own name. It would
be no advantage to have those stones hung around one's
neck while travelling through this country. The Greeks
have never forgiven the British for making off with some
of their most valuable national treasure. It is said that the
first formal request received by every new British ambas-
sador in Athens is for the return of the marbles, and I
speculate that anyone associated with their taking would
be regarded here as piratical. Galt himself, when he wrote
of the 'temptation' being too great, seemed to concede
that removal of the stones was morally suspect.

The marbles venture having come to nought, there was still the possibility of circumventing Napoleon's blockade with an Aegean trading company. My ancestor was impressed with Mykonos, its situation and its people, and elected to establish his new enterprise here. 'In their manners,' he observed, 'the present race of the Myconiots are considered more polite and liberal than the other Greeks. This is ascribed to the influence and example of a Russian Nobleman who resided here as consul-general about five and twenty years ago, with the view of favouring the projects of his Government among the insular Greeks. His lady, a Venetian woman of high birth, introduced balls and theatrical exhibitions, to which all the inhabitants, above the very lowest rank, were freely admitted.' Of the Russian consul, nothing more is said in *Letters from the Levant*.

Galt acquired a building on Mykonos, which he intended to use as a warehouse for the trading company. The building had previously been headquarters for the Russian mission. He describes it briefly: 'On a point of land close to the town stands a large mansion, erected by Count Orloff, and afterwards the residence of the Russian consul-general. . . . The document granting it to me by the community is still in my possession.'

If it has survived, I want to see Galt's building. This is an errand of no consequence, perhaps, yet all of us take such errands seriously from time to time. We examine headstones, sepia photographs, heirlooms, and old buildings, looking for some sign of ourselves, proof that life oversteps a lifetime, evidence that we weren't born yesterday and won't die tomorrow. In a broader sense, our curiosity about ancient and medieval Greece is the same.

I don't have much to go on by way of a physical description – 'on a point of land close to the town stands a large mansion.' Almost certainly, however, there would not have been more than one house built by Count Orloff, nor more than one Russian consular building. Catherine the Great wrested consular rights from the Turks in 1774, but never pushed the privilege to full advantage. The Russian consuls were posted in the islands irregularly and without great resources. My best bet, it seems, rather than searching for physical likenesses of Galt's vague sketch, is to enquire after a house built by the Russians.

In case Count Orloff's mansion is an obvious landmark, though, I spend one day circulating through the town, scouting for points of land and large consular-looking houses. Nothing obvious reveals itself. Instead a scene appears recalling the descriptions, left by my ancestor and others, of the unique mourning practices on Mykonos. Theodore Bent in *The Cyclades*, published in 1884 (probably the best early travel record of these islands), wrote: 'Everywhere in the Cyclades we were told that when we came to Mykonos we should hear the best lamentations over the dead that exist in Greece: that barren Mykonos had this one unenviable speciality; nowhere else could the wailing women sing over the dead such stirring, heart-rending dirges as there. So we went to Mykonos with the firm determination of waiting until somebody died.' Someone did die, and Bent saw and heard the extraordinary Mykoniot laments. Now, a century later, I come upon an open doorway in which sits a priest flanked by two old women. It is a laying out, the body visible in a room behind. Passing and repassing, I listen for the wonderful, wailing dirge, but there is only a faint weeping and occasional muffled moans. Too late, by years or generations. No matter now; time passes, ways change, all things must die.

There may be a scholarly teacher or librarian in town, someone bookish who would know the Russian house. In the library I am shown a picture book about the island, a

pretty piece of work, but it doesn't answer my question.
At the tourist police then, where I go to explain my search
and ask advice, it is decided that I should speak to the
mayor.

On the second floor of an ample old waterfront building
are established the Mykoniot municipal offices. The
mayor, *o dthiemarkos*, receives me cordially in his spacious,
antique chamber, well appointed and well preserved. He
places me in a comfortable chair opposite the mayoral
desk and invites my questions. Although the setting is
formal, our interview is not. The *dthiemarkos* dresses much
as the boatmen in the harbour, and though very self-
assured, he is relaxed and casual. Only one thing disturbs
me about this meeting. Behind the mayor and to one side
stands a large, loutish man with arms folded. Whenever
my Greek falters, he interjects aggressively, assuming the
role of translator for the mayor, except that he doesn't
realize my problem is one of expression, not of understanding, and he employs an unspeakable brand of English. Whether he serves as administrative assistant or as
bodyguard or as a kind of demonic overseer for some
invisible interest group, I can't tell. Despite his interrup-
tions, though, the mayor and I carry on quite coherently.

'This great-great-grandfather of mine,' I explain after a
long and broken preamble, 'acquired a building here on
Mykonos. It was a big house, originally constructed for
the Russian consuls.'

'Yes,' interjects the lout in Greek. 'The Russians took
many of these islands from the Turks, and held them for
many years.' An expert in local history the mayor's
sidekick would be, only his facts are distorted. It is true
that the Russians were in military control of some Aegean
islands between 1770 and 1774, but they never really
occupied them in a colonial sense.

The mayor is smiling. 'Your great-great-grandfather

actually bought the building?' he asks, apparently incredulous. He and his human shadow confer for a moment,
and then they call to a secretary in the anteroom. She
appears with a document which the three of them examine
closely, at length arriving at a mutually agreed upon
conclusion.

'This is the building,' announces the mayor.

'This?' I'm not sure I understand.

'This building,' he repeats emphatically, gesturing
around the room. 'The building we're sitting in now. It
was the house of the Russian consuls. There is no other.
It must be this building.'

'The inhabitants of Myconi,' wrote John Galt, 'have in
their chancery a registry of territorial property, which
extends back many hundreds of years.' It occurs to me to
look at this property register, to see if it confirms the
mayor's reasoning. I ask him where it is. He shrugs, as if
perhaps I'm not taking him at his word, but he telephones
the responsible bureaucrat, giving an explanation I don't
quite catch, then reports that they are very busy in the
property office just now, but if I could wait for a couple
of days. . . . Some uneasiness has crept into the conversation. It is just conceivable they think I'm nursing a
property claim, guarding a yellow deed to the town hall
after all these years and generations.

'*Then birazei*,' I say. It doesn't matter. And add, 'I'm
pleased to find the house.' The mayor smiles, again
relaxed, and we part amicably. Back in the harbour, I look
closely at the building. Downstairs is a taverna where I've
taken some of my meals, and beside the taverna, a
shipping agent. Apart from a few of the newer hotels, this
old mansion appears to be the town's largest structure. It
does fit Galt's loose description, more or less. There is no
reason why it should fit exactly, since he was remembering it from a distance of twenty-three years, the time

between his Greek travels and his autobiography. I see now a worn plaque on the façade recording that the house was erected for the Russian consuls and 'restored by the diligent mayor' of Mykonos in 1922. This is almost certainly right, the piece of real estate on which he staked his doomed commercial dreams. It's an interesting idea, the notion that I might share some legal claim to this property. The mayor was worried for a moment, perhaps over the same fleeting thought. But the answer is not really worth knowing. A man would have to be crazed with greed or mad with ancestor worship to attempt to pry their town hall away from a group of Greek islanders. Imagine the fury! Imagine the impassioned reprisals! Much possible imagining goes with this imaginary claim, and I do spend some time mulling it over and decorating the tale. It is, after all, an exercise in imagination, this quest for the past, and I am well situated to spin it out just now, sitting in the café on the first floor of this very real, unimagined house where John Galt once planned to run Napoleon's blockade.

Wind and rain churn the sea for two days, and then the weather breaks a little. He will take us today. There are just enough passengers and the harbour police have given their approval.

A great swell lingers from the storm and rolls us near to vertical, and back, and then toward the other side, and back, spraying sheets of brine across the deck and passengers. This wild roll forces everyone to grab a rail and stay with it, and leaves two people pale and very sick. The channel is known for rough water, but many travellers cross here just the same. On the other side lies Delos, sacred island of the early Greeks, once the religious and commercial centre of Aegean civilization, now an anti-quarian reserve.

In 540 B.C. it was declared that neither birth nor death should defile this consecrated island, which commandment the ancients obeyed scrupulously. Rheneia, an islet immediately to the west, received the dying and all women about to give birth. Midway between European Greece and Asia Minor, Delos served as a pivotal entrepot and banking centre, as well as the most important religious sanctuary in the Aegean. From across the islands and the mainland Greek pilgrims converged on Delos to worship the ancient gods. Its temples were probably raised with fortunes built on maritime trade, but its reputation as a hallowed place precedes this commercial connection. Apollo, a central deity in pre-classical times, was said to have been born here.

Pythagoras glides past in luminous white robes, on his way to worship at the altar of Apollo where only bloodless sacrifices were made. Pythagoras was right: the wheel of transmigration spins on and on. We too come here to say our prayers, just as they did in the century before the Persian War. We come to worship the dead and all their ruined works, else why come at all, the island being unpeopled now, the grass filled with fallen stones and splintered busts, the treasure gone to Rome, to Venice, to Constantinople, and the wind now blowing, swirling through the empty Delian streets as it would whistle through the cracks of an ancient, plundered tomb, chanting the dark, neutral hymn of human death.

Wander through the streets, planted forever in this barren plate of bedrock, a very small island, traversable in hours, and see the sacred lake, unwatered now and sad; see the great marble shrines – of Dionysius, of Hera, of Poseidon, of the gods of Egypt and Syria – all worn to jumbled stones and dust; and see the Naxian lions, long flayed by the elements and shrunken to gaunt, foetal memories of their former lives. Here and there, in crumbled squares and courtyards, cisterns delve deep below the surface, some secular, others for holy rites, and others still to house the sacred fish. Lie beside one, dropping head and shoulders down, and see who lives on Delos now – enormous prehistoric frogs.

A man climbs the Sacred Way to the height of Mount Kynthus, all of ancient Greece mouldering below, discovers here the ruins of the island's summit temple, an altar to omnipotent greybearded Zeus. Fiercely the wind is raking Delos, wearing all the stones thinner and smoother, and whipping this man's map from his November-cold hands – let it dance away, his journey's almost done. On the slope below, an eerie boulder lies exposed, skull-like, with rows of rectangular dental windcarvings, the teeth of the dead. Holding this ground inviolate, banishing birth and death to another island, they desperately held in check an overwhelming fear: that we live and die, visit the earth and leave it, still the most elusive truth to know. They couldn't foresee that people like me would come in a much later season, living and dying in their place, continuing them and refashioning them just as they refashioned the world of their ancestors in their own time. Now we can make such guesses on hilltops such as this, because they went before, and so move a little closer to some sense of our beginning, and our end.

An invitation to slip back close to the beginning and look less doomfully toward the end. This is the legacy of recorded Greek history, and anyone scaling Mount Kynthus must receive some whisper of the gift. Time and all time's monuments: we are dwarfed by the thought, and at the same time we are enlarged. I'm thinking up here of the two ghosts travelling near me this year, the shaman-philosopher Pythagoras and the provincial novelist John Galt. As he perhaps intended, Pythagoras remains a puzzle, engulfed in his own mystique, obscure, labyrinthine, seductive. Pythagoras knew truths we have forgotten, secrets about the earth and our attachment to it, that make him a giant totem figure, a seer beyond our ken. We could retrieve him, of course. From time to time, I've tried to resurrect him here. He's not really beyond our ken, only beyond the world we have constructed and choose to inhabit, a world framed by the mathematics he helped discover, but set apart from the magic oneness he divined. Pythagoras could be the spaceman from another galaxy who descends on coils of invisible energy to give us the secret of creation. We are astounded by his presence, and especially by his technological superiority, and our fascination draws us near, but instead of receiving and unravelling the ultimate message, we ask him for his transportation formula. Our world is, and has been for centuries, more interested in the seminal mathematics of Pythagoras than in his metaphysics. We have pulled him apart, with the help of Aristotle's pincers, and amputated a body of thought which was once all of a piece. Pythagoras would add that we've pulled ourselves apart, cut ourselves off from the heart of the matter, the eternal pulse of the earth or, in his terms, the soul of all things.

He came to worship here, it is said, continuing to pay lip service to the ancient Greek pantheon on Delos while cultivating his own idiosyncratic religious views. Of all the thinkers, statesmen, generals, merchants and priests who reached the sacred island over many centuries from everywhere on the Mediterranean littoral, I can't think of anyone I'd rather snatch a moment's conversation with than the great magus-philosopher of the 6th century B.C. Perhaps that wish stems partly from his intriguing wordlessness, none of his writings having survived. Then again, I'd also like to speak with that other ghost, John Galt, whose words survive in such quantity that I've never read them all. Both ghosts have travelled silently with me long enough now that I'd like them to step out of the shadows for a moment and tell me how I'm doing. We are always judging the past. Occasionally we stop short and wonder how it might judge us.

My ancestor stirs no great reverence in me, but I do admire his accomplishments, and profit, perhaps, from his literary company. Pythagoras, by means of a far-reaching mind, travelled from the centre of the earth out to the farthest stars and back to fruit-laden Samos, describing magic triangles in the sky. John Galt's voyages were more mundane, more tangible, more like my own, although he came across scenes I'll never witness, and travelled with hardships I'll never have to bear, large inconveniences like Napoleon's war, murderous Mediterranean freebooters, and the vagaries of transport by sail. Once, while sleeping under a tree, his party had valuable gear stolen, including a horse, by Anatolian robbers. Those were lawless times in the Levant – fifty years later a group of British travellers was seized for ransom by brigands and later slaughtered. Galt was not always as observant as a reader now would like him to have been, but he did have the courage to go and the diligence to write a record. In these days of island hopping by hovercraft and instant telecommunications, his slow sea voyage and long, unhurried letters home seem worth remembering.

Here at the Delian high-point, while I can imagine a few parting words from Pythagoras, I can't see my ancestor anywhere. Galt, as he conceded in his book, was impatient with desolation and not much taken with ruins. Although attentive to history, he was above all a creature of his own time, a believer in science, commercial growth, material progress. The past was something to be overcome. Pythagoras, on the other hand, would feel a strong affinity for this abandoned island, and for all the other vacant lots that Greek time has given us. He's here now to break the silence, dressed in the billowing white cassock of ancient Greek priests, fleshy and real, but at the same time faceless.

'It's as I foresaw,' he reflects, gazing down across acres of broken marble grandeur. 'The thundering footsteps of time all stopped dead in their tracks.' We can see the whole of Delos easily from where we stand.

'The world is a music box,' he continues. 'Each of us turns the key in his time. Each reclaims the silence. Always the music plays. You can hear it now, even on Delos, even after seven cycles of neglect.'

I've forgotten what the number seven signifies. It doesn't matter. Reality by numbers isn't my game. But I do hear the wind siffling around this hill, and the eternal rhythm of the Delian sea below.

'The earth marries itself,' he intones, beginning to fade. 'The earth embalms itself. The earth is reborn.'

He's gone, leaving a sense of Pythagorean infinity locked inside all these old stones. A great city falls to ruin, but a ruin lasts forever. Or will the sea rise one winter and swallow Delos, grinding down these corridors of cracked majesty to granules of fine white sand? The earth embalms itself, yet the sacred island bears witness to centuries of unquenchable life. Even here on Delos the earth intends to be reborn.